THE JOSSEY-BASS ACADEMIC ADMINISTRATOR'S GUIDE TO

Exemplary Leadership

The Jossey-Bass Academic Administrator's Guides are designed to help new and experienced campus professionals when a promotion or move brings on new responsibilities, new tasks, and new situations. Each book focuses on a single topic, exploring its application to the higher education setting. These real-world guides provide advice about day-to-day responsibilities as well as an orientation to the organizational environment of campus administration. From department chairs to office staff supervisors, these concise resources will help college and university administrators understand and overcome obstacles to success.

We hope you will find this volume useful in your work. To that end, we welcome your reaction to this volume and to the series in general, including suggestions for future topics.

THE JOSSEY-BASS

ACADEMIC ADMINISTRATOR'S
GUIDE TO

Exemplary Leadership

JAMES M. KOUZES

BARRY Z. POSNER

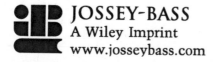

JOSSEY-BASS
A Wiley Imprint
www.josseybass.com

Published by Jossey-Bass
A Wiley Imprint
989 Market Street, San Francisco, CA 94103-1741   www.josseybass.com

Jossey-Bass books and products are available through most bookstores. To contact Jossey-Bass directly call our Customer Care Department within the U.S. at 800-956-7739, outside the U.S. at 317-572-3986 or fax 317-572-4002.

Jossey-Bass also publishes its books in a variety of electronic formats. Some content that appears in print may not be available in electronic books.

Library of Congress Cataloging-in-Publication Data

Kouzes, James M., 1945–
    The Jossey-Bass academic administrator's guide to exemplary leadership / James M. Kouzes, Barry Z. Posner.—1st ed.
        p.   cm.
Includes bibliographical references and index.
    ISBN 978-0-7879-6664-5
    1. Education, Higher—Adminstration—Handbooks, manuals, etc.   2. Educational leadership—Handbooks, manuals, etc.   I. Title: Academic administrator's guide to exemplary leadership.
II. Posner, Barry Z.   III. Title.
    LB2341.K68 2003
    378.1'11—dc21

                                                                                    2002156563

PB Printing   10 9 8 7

CONTENTS

PREFACE

The *Jossey-Bass Academic Administrator's Guide to Exemplary Leadership* is about how college and university leaders mobilize others to want to get extraordinary things done. It's about the practices leaders use to transform values into actions, visions into realities, obstacles into innovations, separateness into solidarity, and risks into rewards. It's about leadership that creates the climate in which people together turn challenging opportunities into remarkable successes. And there are certainly no shortages of challenging opportunities in higher education. In fact, the opportunities for leadership are available to everyone, every day.

WHO SHOULD READ THIS BOOK?

The fundamental purpose of this guidebook to leading is to assist people throughout the higher education community in furthering their abilities to lead others to get extraordinary things done. From individual faculty member to department chair, program director to dean, through vice president to president, leadership matters. Likewise from the staff and managers of residential life offices, career development, student records, admissions, campus safety, information technology, library, counseling, physical plant, alumni relations, and development, among others, leadership matters. We have written this book to help you—no matter your position on campus—develop your capacity to guide others to places they have never been before. We believe you are capable of developing yourself as a leader far more than tradition has ever assumed possible.

This book is not about being in a leadership *position* (as if leadership was a place) but about having the courage and spirit to move from whatever place you are in to making a significant difference. This book is not about leaders *per se;* nor is it about the few, the rarefied celebrities of academe. It is about leadership and how ordinary people exercise it—and in the process become leaders. In it, we present stories of regular people on college campuses and university settings who got bigger-than-life results. In it, we offer practical guidance for enhancing your leadership capabilities.

RESEARCH-BASED PRACTICES

While the *Jossey-Bass Academic Administrator's Guide to Exemplary Leadership* is written to strengthen your abilities and uplift your spirits, the principles and practices described in it are based solidly in quantitative and qualitative research. The book has its origins in a study we began in 1983. We wanted to know what people did when they were at their "personal best" in leading others. These were experiences in which, in their own perception, people set their individual leadership standards of excellence. We started with an assumption that we didn't have to interview and survey star performers to discover best practices. Instead, we assumed that by asking ordinary people to describe extraordinary experiences, we would be able to find and identify patterns of success. And we surely did.

The results of our initial investigation—and of the continuing research we have conducted for two decades, including the projects we initiated in preparing specifically for exploring and understanding leadership in higher education—have been striking both in their refutation of many leader stereotypes and in their consistency. Leaders do exhibit certain distinct practices when they are doing their best. And this pattern of behavior varies little from industry to industry, profession to profession, community to community, country to country. And, as we found out in our most recent round of research, it is consistent over time. We've asked leaders the same question being asked of us: "What's new, and what's different?"

Leaders everywhere and of every age told us that the fundamentals of leadership are the same today as they were in the 1980s and the 1990s, and they probably have been the same for centuries. In that sense, nothing's new. Leadership is not a fad. It's a fact. It's not here today, gone tomorrow. It's here today and here forever. True, the context has changed a bit over time, but leadership remains as an understandable and a universal process. While each leader is a unique individual, there are patterns to the practice of leadership that are shared.

A FIELD GUIDE FOR LEADERS

Think of this volume as a field guide to take along on your leadership journey. We have designed it to describe what leaders do, explain the fundamental principles that support these leadership practices, provide actual case examples of real people on college and university campuses who demonstrate each practice, and offer specific recommendations on what you can do to make these practices your own and to continue your development as a leader. It offers a set of leadership practices that are based on the real-world experiences of thousands of people who have answered the call for leadership.

Chapter One introduces you to our point of view about leadership and describes the Five Practices of Exemplary Leadership® revealed in our research. In it we also describe the characteristics that people most admire in their leaders. We present to you the foundation on which all great leadership is built. We tell the leadership story from the inside and move outward, describing leadership first as a personal journey of exploration and then as a rallying of others. Our research has shown that leadership is not the private reserve of a few charismatic men and women. It is a process ordinary people use when they are bringing forth the best from themselves and others. Liberate the leader in everyone and extraordinary things happen.

In Chapters Two through Six we explore the Five Practices, one to a chapter. The discussions are built on the results of our research, and we expand our understanding of leadership by drawing on the research of other scholars. We do not summarize the literature on leadership or the various concepts of leadership; instead, we provide a particular point of view on leading that is empirically sound and practically valuable. We illustrate each practice with case examples and recommended actions you can take to put the practice to use. There is no sacred order to these chapters. We recommend that you read Chapter One and then go wherever your interests are. There is no one best way. Please remember though that all of these practices are essential. While you might skip around in this book, you can't skip any of the fundamentals of leadership.

Finally, in Chapter Seven, we discuss how leadership is a learnable set of practices, accessible to anyone. We show you that leadership is everyone's business and that the first place to look for leadership is within yourself. In so doing we hope to demystify leadership and show how each of us has the capacity to lead. We talk about the contrasts and contradictions of leadership—no one ever said leadership would be easy—and how you can learn to strike a balance and not overdo. We offer guidance on how you can continue your own growth and development, offering a secret for success in life.

If you want to know more about how we conducted our research for this book, you'll find detailed information on our research methodology, statistical data, and highlights of validation studies by other scholars on our web site: www.theleadershipchallenge.com. Those interested in a more thorough treatment of the Five Practices of Exemplary Leadership model, and its application across a wide variety of organizational settings, should read *The Leadership Challenge* (3rd edition, Jossey-Bass, 2002).

There is a core theme that weaves its way through all the chapters of this book. Wherever we are, the message we keep hearing is this: *leadership is a relationship.* Whether it's one-to-one or one-to-many, leadership is a relationship between those who aspire to lead and those who chose to follow. Young or old, faculty or staff, manager or individual contributor, experienced or novice, success in leadership and success in life will continue to be a function of how well we work and get along with one another.

Preface

THE FUTURE OF LEADERSHIP

The domain of leaders is the future. We hope this book contributes to the revitalization of higher education—its people and its institutions—to the renewal of healthy college communities, and to greater respect and understanding among people of all traditions. We also fervently hope that it enriches your life and the lives of your students, colleagues, alumni, friends, and family. The most significant contribution leaders make is to the long-term development of people and institutions so they can adapt, prosper, and grow.

Beyond all of this, we want to convince you that leadership matters not just in your own career and within your own university. It's important in every sector, in every community, and in every country. Right now we need more leaders, and we need them more than ever. There is so much extraordinary work to be done. We need leaders who can unite us and ignite us.

In the end, we realize that leadership development is ultimately self-development. Meeting the leadership challenge is a personal—and a daily—challenge for all of us.

ACKNOWLEDGMENTS

There's always a long list of people to thank and credit when anything special is accomplished, and well there should be. Leadership is not a solo performance, nor is writing about it.

First, we once again acknowledge and give thanks to the scores of folks who have been with us over the past two decades and more than a dozen leadership projects, programs, and publications. We devoted nearly four pages to mentioning their names in the acknowledgment section of *The Leadership Challenge* (3rd edition) and continue to carry a deep debt of gratitude for their gracious support and encouragement.

Second, we want to recognize a number of special people connected with this particular volume. Jan Hunter continued as our developmental editor, once again gracefully sharpening our focus, clarifying concepts and applications, and quieting our loquaciousness. Thanks to David Brightman, the Higher and Adult Education series editor at Jossey-Bass, who championed this project and kept the pressure on us to produce a timely volume concentrated on the needs of the higher education audience. Our Jossey-Bass product manager Lisa Shannon helped us balance this project with others and continues to encourage our hearts through both her enthusiasm and her demands. The external reviews of Gale Erlandson, Charles Slater, and Jodi Levine Laufgraben were of exceptional service in directing our attention to the needs of higher education and in providing specific practical and reflective directions. The continuing administrative support of Ellen Peterson, along with her cheery countenance, helped to keep every nit from becoming a distraction.

The final list of acknowledgments is literally unending. Here's to every faculty member, university staff member, scores of college administrators, as well as countless students, who contributed directly and indirectly to whatever we know, and have learned, about leading in higher education settings and situations. You taught us when we experimented, when we tried and succeeded, and when we missed the mark and needed to try again. Whatever we learned and accomplished, we couldn't have done it alone. Many thanks. And, by the way, for those of you who know us, we're not done!

Santa Clara, California
March 2003

James M. Kouzes
Barry Z. Posner

ABOUT THE AUTHORS

J*im Kouzes and Barry Posner* have been involved with higher education administration for the past three decades.

Jim founded the Joint Center for Human Services Development at San Jose State University and directed the Executive Development Center at Santa Clara University. He's currently an Executive Fellow at the Center for Innovation and Entrepreneurship at the Leavey School of Business, Santa Clara University. Jim can be reached at (877) 866-9691, extension 239, or via e-mail at jim@kouzesposner.com.

Barry is currently dean of the Leavey School of Business and professor of leadership. He has served previously as associate dean for Graduate Programs and managing partner for Executive Education at Santa Clara University, and has held other campus leadership positions. Barry can be reached at (408) 554-4523, or via e-mail at bposner@scu.edu.

Jim and Barry received the prestigious Wilbur M. McFeely Award, given to the nation's top leadership educators, by the International Management Council in 2001. They have provided leadership education programs on college campuses across the United States and the globe, including such schools as California State University (Northridge, Sacramento, Sonoma), Cornerstone University, Curtain University, DeAnza-Foothill Community College District, Gavilan Community College, Harvard College, Kent State University, North Texas State University, Queen's University, Simon Fraser University, Stanford University, Universidad Francisco Marroquin, University of California (Riverside, San

Diego, Santa Cruz), University of Dayton, University of Denver, University of Massachusetts (Amherst), University of Minnesota, University of Saskatchewan, University of South Carolina, University of Southern Maine, University of Texas (Austin, El Paso), University of Western Australia, Western New England College, and Willamette University. They have also conducted workshops and made keynote presentations for the Association to Advance Collegiate Schools of Business (AACSB) International, Association of Fraternity Advisors, California Business-Higher Education Forum, Canadian Association of University Business Officers, Community College League of California, National Association for Campus Activities, National Association of Student Personnel Administrators, Pacific Association of College Registrars and Admissions Officers, and the Western Association of College and University Business Officers.

Jim and Barry are coauthors of the award-winning book *The Leadership Challenge*, which has been a selection of the Macmillan Executive Book Club and the Fortune Book Club. It won the James A. Hamilton Hospital Administrators' Book of the Year Award, the Critics' Choice Award, and been a *Business Week* bestseller. Their book *Credibility: How Leaders Gain and Lose It, Why People Demand It* was chosen by *Industry Week* as one of the ten best management books. They have also collaborated on *Encouraging the Heart: A Leader's Guide to Rewarding and Recognizing Others* and *The Leadership Challenge Planner*. Based on solid research involving over 200,000 surveys, 4,200 written case studies, and 150 in-depth interviews, these books describe the leadership principles and practices that generate extraordinary performance in individuals and organizations.

Jim and Barry also developed the widely used and highly acclaimed *Leadership Practices Inventory (LPI)*, a 360-degree questionnaire assessing leadership behavior. The LPI has been administered to over 250,000 individuals, and over one million observers have provided feedback using the LPI. An online (web-based) version is available, as is a student version. Over 175 doctoral dissertations and academic research projects have been based on their Five Practices of Exemplary Leadership® model. For more on all of Jim and Barry's publications and this research, visit www.theleadershipchallenge.com.

1

Leadership Is a Relationship

IN OVER TWENTY YEARS OF RESEARCH, we've been fortunate to have heard and read the stories of thousands of ordinary people who've led others to get extraordinary things done. These are not especially famous people nor are they likely to be featured in the popular press. They're people much like the people you run into every day, across campus and across town. We've chosen to tell the stories of some of these everyday leaders because we firmly believe that—at its core—leadership is not about position or title. It's about caring, about relationships, and about what you *do*.

We firmly believe that leadership is an identifiable set of skills and practices that are available to each of us, not just a few charismatic men and women. We challenge the myth that leadership is something found only at the highest levels of the organization, whether it's the corporate executive suite or the halls of academe. The theory that there are only a *few* great men and women who can lead us to greatness is just plain wrong. We consider the women and men in our research to be great, and so do those with whom they've worked. It's because there are so many— not so few—leaders that people are able to get extraordinary things done on a regular basis, even in extraordinary times.

We know, through our research, experience, and readings that ordinary people can learn how to get extraordinary things done. To us this is inspiring. It gives us great hope for the future. Hope, because it means that no one need wait around to be saved by someone riding in on a white horse. Hope, because there's no shortage of leaders on campus searching for the opportunities to make a difference.

There's another crucial truth about leadership, one that we've known for a long time and have come to prize even more these days. In talking to leaders and studying their cases, we see a very clear message woven into every situation and every action: *leadership is a relationship*. Leadership is a relationship between those who aspire to lead and those who choose to follow.

Evidence abounds for this point of view. For instance, in examining the critical variables for success in the top three jobs in large organizations, Jodi Taylor and her colleagues at the Center for Creative Leadership found the number one success factor to be "relationships with subordinates" (Taylor, personal communication, April 1998). The critical importance of understanding and interacting with others is underscored in higher education settings. In *Leadership Reconsidered* the authors note that while most institutions of higher learning are organized and governed according to two seemingly contradictory sets of practices (hierarchical and individualistic models), the requirement for any meaningful change is developing positive working relationships (Astin and Astin, 2000). Even in this nanosecond world of e-everything, that conclusion is consistent with the facts. In an online survey, respondents were asked to indicate, among other things, which would be more essential to organizational success in five years—social skills or skills in using the Internet. Seventy-two percent selected social skills; 28 percent, Internet skills ("FC Roper Starch Survey," 1999). Internet literati completing a poll online realize that it's not the web of technology that matters the most, it's the web of people. Social capital joins intellectual and financial capital as the necessary pillars for institutional greatness.

Similar results were found in a study by Public Allies, an AmeriCorps organization dedicated to creating young leaders who can strengthen their communities. Public Allies sought the opinions of eighteen- to thirty-year-olds on the subject of leadership. Among the items was a question about the qualities that were important in a good leader. Topping the respondents' list is "Being able to see a situation from someone else's point of view"; in second place, "Getting along well with other people" (Public Allies, 1998).

Success in leadership and success in life has been, is now, and will continue to be a function of how well people work and get along with one another. Success in leading will be wholly dependent upon the capacity to build and sustain those human relationships that enable people to get extraordinary things done on a regular basis.

THE FIVE PRACTICES OF EXEMPLARY LEADERSHIP

In conducting research on personal-best leadership experiences, we've discovered that leaders mobilize others to get extraordinary things done in virtually every arena of organized activity. We've found examples in higher education, profit-based and nonprofit firms, manufacturing and services, government, schools, businesses, the armed forces, health care, entertainment, and community service. Leaders reside in every college campus, city and country, in every position and every place. They're employees and volunteers, young and old, women and men. Leadership knows no racial or religious bounds, no ethnic or cultural borders. We find exemplary leadership everywhere we look.

We've discovered that people who guide others along pioneering journeys follow rather similar paths. Though each case is unique in expression, each path is marked by some common patterns of action. We've forged these common practices into a model of leadership, and we offer it here as guidance for leaders as they attempt to keep their own bearings and guide others toward peak achievements. When getting extraordinary things done, leaders:

- Model the way

- Inspire a shared vision

- Challenge the process

- Enable others to act

- Encourage the heart

These Five Practices of Exemplary Leadership—which we discuss briefly in this chapter and then in depth in later chapters—aren't the private property of the people we studied or of a few select shining stars. They're available to anyone, in any collegiate organization or situation, who accepts the leadership challenge. And they're widely applicable and tested. Numerous scholars have applied the Five Practices of Exemplary Leadership framework to their investigation of leadership in higher education; several even began with the personal-best leadership case study approach. For example, from studies of college coaches (Elliott, 1990; Coffman, 1999) to presidents (Bauer, 1993), vice presidents (Plowman, 1991), business and finance officers (Stephenson, 2002), and deans and department chairs (Xu, 1991), scholars have found these practices closely correlated with leadership effectiveness and satisfaction. Further, researchers have found few significant differences between the leadership practices of those in higher education and those outside of higher education.

These practices are not the accident of a special moment in history. They've stood the test of time. Our most recent research confirms that they're just as relevant—if not more relevant—today as they were when we first began our investigation.

Model the Way

Titles are granted, but it's your behavior that wins you respect. Exemplary leaders know that if they want to gain commitment and achieve the highest standards, they must be models of the behavior they expect of others. "It's as straightforward," career services director Andy Ceperley told us, "as never asking anyone else to do something you're not willing to do yourself." Leaders *model the way*.

Andy had served in career services positions at the University of Virginia, University of Texas, and Santa Clara University—experiencing a wide variety of academic institutions: public and private, secular and nonsecular, centralized and decentralized. Then he was asked by the vice president of student affairs at a neighboring university to help their career center deal with implementing an "internship guarantee" for every student. The center had experienced great staff turnover and burned out more than one director. Andy told us that he had to get "personally very deep into conversations with people on campus. I interviewed over fifty people and asked tons of questions. I was all over the campus, with students, faculty, staff, and alumni." In the process, he needed to be able to listen attentively to people's perceptions of career services and how a service organization engages with the campus: "It's an enterprise of relationship building because no one really has to use our services. My job was to summarize the feedback and offer solutions to reduce the center's credibility gap." One year after the study the career center is in a growth mode with a new director, new facility, and a strengthened portfolio of student programs.

To effectively model the behavior they expect of others, as Andy points out, means that leaders must first be clear about their guiding principles. Leaders must find their own voice and clearly and distinctively give voice to their values. Since leaders are supposed to stand up for their beliefs, they'd better have some beliefs to stand up for.

Eloquent speeches about common values, however, aren't nearly enough. Leaders' deeds are far more important than their words when determining how serious they really are about what they say. Words and deeds must be consistent. Exemplary leaders go first. They go first by setting the example through daily actions that demonstrate they are deeply committed to their beliefs. Leaders, as Andy's experience demonstrates, understand the power of spending time with people, of working side by side with colleagues, of telling stories that make the values come alive, of being highly visible during times of uncertainty, and of asking questions to get people to think about aspirations and priorities.

Inspire a Shared Vision

Leaders have a desire to make something happen, to change the way things are, to create something that no one else has ever created before. In some ways, leaders live their lives backward. They see pictures in their mind's eye of what the results will look like even before they've started their project, much as an architect draws a blueprint or an engineer builds a model. Their clear image of the future pulls them forward. Yet visions seen only by leaders are insufficient to create an organized movement or a significant change. A person with no constituents is not a leader, and people will not follow until they accept a vision as their own. Therefore, leaders must *inspire a shared vision*.

Lillas Brown joined the Business and Leadership Programs, Extension Division, at the University of Saskatchewan following a career in retailing. It took some time, she told us, for academics (the faculty) to appreciate what she might have to contribute to their effectiveness as department heads. There was little doubt in her mind, however, that with patience, great listening, and perseverance, she'd be able to enlist the faculty administrators on her campus in a common leadership vision. She knew that faculty would respond positively to articulating shared values around teaching, scholarship, and service.

To enlist people in a vision, leaders must know their constituents and speak their language. Lillas, like others we interviewed, knew that people must believe that leaders understand their needs and have their interests at heart before they will come on board. Leaders breathe life into the hopes and dreams of others and enable them to see the exciting possibilities that the future holds. Leaders forge a unity of purpose by showing constituents how the dream is for the common good. Leaders ignite the flame of passion in others by expressing enthusiasm for the compelling vision of their group, communicating their passion through vivid language and an expressive style.

Challenge the Process

Leaders are pioneers—people who are willing to step out into the unknown. They search for opportunities to innovate, grow, and improve. Every single personal-best leadership case we collected involved some change from the status quo. Not one person claimed to have achieved a personal best by keeping things the same. All leaders *challenge the process.*

But leaders aren't the only creators or originators of new curricula, programs, services, or processes. In fact, it's more likely that they're not: innovation comes more from listening than from telling. The leader's primary contribution is in the recognition of good ideas, the support of those ideas, and the willingness to challenge the system to get new products, processes, services, and systems adopted. It might be more accurate, then, to say that leaders are *early adopters* of innovation.

Associate Professor Patrick Murphy, C.M., didn't come up with the original idea for a public services graduate program at DePaul University. But he listened to the aspirations being espoused by the university's president and the yearnings of many students in the college about wanting to apply the lessons being learned in their communities (not just corporations). He also heard several of his colleagues express interest in being involved with a program that intersected the private and public sectors and how there seemed to be opportunities to apply best practices to community-based organizations. When he first presented his ideas to his dean, the negative response was couched in financial limitations and limiting priorities. Not easily discouraged, Pat shopped the idea around the campus—in the process violating several campus governance taboos (both horizontally and vertically)—before finding support from the trustees and turning a sleepy little program into the largest graduate program in the college.

In less than five years the number of students in the program doubled, two satellite campuses were added to the program, along with courses being offered abroad in two countries. Pat paid for much of it by creating a small consulting and executive training business (still another story about challenging the process!). He also launched several fundraising programs, including a "Pub Night" to raise scholarship money for students studying in Ireland. Many of these achievements he had to bring in "under the radar"—to keep from attracting too much attention from the central administration.

Leaders, like Pat, know well that innovation and change all involve experimentation, risk, and failure. They proceed anyway. One way of dealing with the potential risks and failures of experimentation is to approach change through incremental steps and small wins. Little victories, when piled on top of each other, build confidence that even the biggest challenges can be met. In so doing, they strengthen commitment to the long-term future.

It would be ridiculous to assert that those who fail over and over again eventually succeed as leaders. Success in any endeavor isn't a process of simply buying enough lottery tickets. The key that unlocks the door to opportunity is learning. Leaders learn from their failures as well as from their successes.

Enable Others to Act

Grand dreams don't become significant realities through the actions of a single person. Leadership is a team effort. Exemplary leaders *enable others to act*. They foster collaboration and build trust. This sense of teamwork goes far beyond a few direct reports or close confidants. Leaders engage all those who must make the project work—and in some way, all who must live with the results—which was precisely the conclusion Charlie Slater reached when recounting his personal-best leadership experience of starting a new doctoral program at the University of the Incarnate Word in San Antonio, Texas. When asked who the leader was in the development of the program, he answered, "There was not a single leader, but rather, there were many leaders. At different times in the process each one was critical. The program would probably not have come about without the leadership of all of these people."

Leaders make it possible for others to do good work. They know that those who are expected to produce the results must feel a sense of personal power and ownership. Charlie talked about how the university president enabled the dean, who in turn enabled Charlie and his colleagues, who in turn worked together with a myriad of other faculty colleagues within the school (on the Curriculum Committee, Faculty Senate, and Board of Trustees) to bring this new program to life. His experience underscored how commitment-and-support leadership has replaced the command-and-control techniques of previous generations. Leaders work to make people feel strong, capable, and committed. Leaders enable others not by hoarding the power they have but by giving it away. The president of the University of the Incarnate Word could not have made the program a reality by himself, and, in fact, no single person or group could have advocated successfully for the program without the cooperation of others. Working together, exemplary leaders strengthen everyone's capacity to deliver on the possibilities they imagine and the promises they make.

In the cases we analyzed, leaders like Charlie proudly discussed teamwork, trust, and empowerment as essential elements of their efforts. Constituents neither perform at their best nor stick around for very long if their leader makes them feel weak, dependent, or alienated. But when a leader makes people feel strong and capable—as if they can do more than they ever thought possible—they'll give it their all and exceed their own expectations. When leadership is a relationship founded on trust and confidence, people take risks, make changes, and keep organizations and movements alive. Through that relationship, leaders turn their constituents into leaders themselves.

Encourage the Heart

Leaders *encourage the heart* of their constituents to carry on, to continue even when they might be tempted to give up. Genuine acts of caring—whether exhibited in dramatic gestures or simple actions—uplift the spirits and draw people forward.

An award for the outstanding faculty member used to be given each year in the Leavey School of Business (Santa Clara University). In those days, Barry Posner was a faculty member and "could never understand how there could be one award, with so many disciplines and, given each discipline's different standards, how it could be determined what 'most outstanding' meant." So, when Barry became dean, "I was determined we'd change the system and do more to recognize the excellence among our faculty. Working with our Council of Chairs, we determined a set of standards (across teaching, scholarship, and service), which were appropriate to all disciplines and all ranks. Any faculty member who could meet (or exceed) all three thresholds would be, in any of our minds, 'extraordinary' and that's what we called the award. We could all be proud of any one of us who could be outstanding across these three performance categories." In the first year, six Extraordinary Faculty awards were granted; five years later, thirteen were awarded. Barry says, "I think it's great that the standards haven't changed, but the behavior (hence the performance) of our faculty has risen to the ideal we set. With this award, we've taken a giant step in eliminating competition among ourselves for 'who's the best?' and now we collectively focus on what each of us needs to do to be best."

It is, after all, part of the leader's job to show appreciation for people's contributions and to create a culture of celebration. Over the years, we've seen thousands of examples of individual recognition and group celebration, from handwritten thank-you notes to marching bands and "This Is Your Life" ceremonies. Yet recognition and celebration aren't simply about fun and games, though both abound when people encourage the hearts of their constituents. Neither are they about pretentious ceremonies designed to create some phony sense of camaraderie. Encouragement is curiously serious business. It's how leaders visibly and behaviorally link rewards with performance. When striving to raise quality standards, recover from disaster, or make dramatic change of any kind, leaders make sure people see the benefit of behavior that's aligned with cherished values. And leaders also know that celebrations and rituals, when done with authenticity and from the heart, build a strong sense of collective identity and community spirit that can carry a group through tough times.

CONSTITUENTS: THE OTHER SIDE OF THE LEADERSHIP STORY

Model the way, inspire a shared vision, challenge the process, enable others to act, and encourage the heart: these are the leadership practices of exemplary leaders. But these practices paint only a partial picture, one that can be complete and vivid only when we add in what constituents expect from their leaders. Leadership is a reciprocal process between those who aspire to lead and those who choose to follow. Any discussion of leadership must attend to the dynamics of this relationship. Strategies, tactics, skills, and techniques are empty without an understanding of the fundamental human aspirations that connect leaders and constituents.

To balance our understanding of leadership, we've asked people what they look for and admire in a leader—what personal values, traits, and characteristics are most important to them in an individual they would *willingly* follow. Responses from more than 100,000 respondents, in higher education and in every industry, and in countries across the globe, affirm and enrich the picture that emerged from our studies of personal bests. Clearly, those who aspire to lead must embrace their constituents' expectations.

WHAT PEOPLE LOOK FOR AND ADMIRE IN THEIR LEADERS

Our survey results have been striking in their regularity over the years. Clearly a person must pass several essential tests before others are willing to grant the title *leader,* as demonstrated by the data presented in Table 1.1.

Although all characteristics receive some votes, and therefore each is important to some people, what is most striking and most evident is that, consistently over time and across continents, *only four* have continuously received over 50 percent of the votes. Some of the other qualities have flirted with consensus, but what people *most* look for and admire in a leader has been constant. As the data clearly show, for people to follow someone *willingly,* the majority of constituents must believe the leader is

- Honest

- Forward-looking

- Competent

- Inspiring

Maybe you'd expect those within higher education to be different than other populations? Well, think again. Responses from hundreds of faculty members (many of them department chairs, associate deans, and deans) over the past few years reaffirm these findings. Comparisons with college student personnel administrators, registrars, and development officers, among other groups of college administrators, are strikingly similar to the faculty and to those from the larger data base.*

Interestingly enough, we asked students to apply this same list of characteristics to their best teachers and found the top four were identical! Who'd want to take a course from someone who wasn't competent or wasn't very excited about the subject matter? How about an instructor

*For a more complete discussion of our research and methodology see *The Leadership Challenge* (3rd edition), Chapter Two, and our web site: www.theleadershipchallenge.com.

who's always changing the syllabus (standards and assignments) and therefore can't be entirely trusted (isn't perceived as honest)? The best teachers, explained students, were able to get them to see the "big picture" and
how these lessons (knowledge, skills, applications) would be beneficial in

Table 1.1. Characteristics of Admired Leaders

Characteristic	Percentage of Respondents Selecting That Characteristic
HONEST	88
FORWARD-LOOKING	71
COMPETENT	66
INSPIRING	65
Intelligent	47
Fair-minded	42
Broad-minded	40
Supportive	35
Straightforward	34
Dependable	33
Cooperative	28
Determined	24
Imaginative	23
Ambitious	21
Courageous	20
Caring	20
Mature	17
Loyal	14
Self-controlled	8
Independent	6

Note: These percentages represent respondents from six continents:
Africa, North America, South America, Asia, Europe, and Australia. The
majority are from the United States. Since we asked people to select
seven characteristics, the total adds up to about 700 percent.

their future. Clearly, our best teachers aren't "lost" and express well their sense of direction (forward-looking).

These investigations of admired leader attributes reveal consistent and clear relationships with the stories we heard people tell us about their personal-best leadership experiences. The Five Practices of Exemplary Leadership and the characteristics of admired leaders are complementary perspectives on the same subject. When they're performing at their peak, leaders are doing more than just getting results. They're also responding to the expectations of their constituents, underscoring the point that leadership is a relationship and that the relationship is one of service to a purpose and to people. As we weave the themes of being honest, forward-looking, competent, and inspiring into the text of the subsequent chapters on the practices, you'll see in more detail how exemplary leaders respond to the needs of their constituents.

CREDIBILITY IS THE FOUNDATION OF LEADERSHIP

The characteristics people look for in those they would willingly follow have remained constant during two decades of growth and recession, booms and busts in college-age students, increasing diversity, passions surrounding affirmative action, focus on student learning outcomes and assessments, the birth of the World Wide Web, the ever-changing political environment, the rising costs of higher education, the expanding focus of collegiate sports (including the growth in women's programs), and the continuing significance of endowments and fundraising efforts for public as well as private institutions (Guskin and Marcy, 2002).

The relative importance of the most desired qualities has varied somewhat over time, but there has been no change in the fact that the four qualities—honest, forward-looking, competent, and inspiring—are what people want most in their leaders. Whether leaders are true to these values is another matter, but what people would like from them has remained constant.

This list of four consistent findings is useful in and of itself—and there's a more profound implication revealed by our research. These key characteristics make up what social psychologists and communications experts refer to as *credibility*. In assessing such questions as why are some people more believable than others, how are reputations formed, how are opinion leaders created, and why are role models adopted, researchers—from scholarly traditions outside the leadership arena—have demonstrated that the key dimensions of credibility and the characteristics of our most admired leaders are remarkably similar. What we've discovered is that more than anything, *people want leaders who are credible.*

People must be able to believe in leaders, that their word can be trusted, that they'll do what they say, that they're personally excited and enthusiastic about the direction in which the group is headed, and that they have the knowledge and skill to lead. Because this finding has been so pervasive and so consistent, we've come to refer to it as The First Law of Leadership: If you don't believe in the messenger, you won't believe the message.

WHAT IS CREDIBILITY BEHAVIORALLY?

Credibility is the foundation of leadership. Our data confirm this assertion time and time again. But what is credibility behaviorally? How do you know it when you see it? Here are some of the common phrases people have used to describe credibility:

- "Leaders practice what they preach."

- "They walk the talk."

- "Their actions are consistent with their words."

- "They put their money where their mouth is."

- "They follow through on their promises."

- *"They do what they say they will do."*

That last is the most frequent response. When it comes to deciding whether a leader is believable, people first listen to the words, then they watch the actions. A judgment of "credible" is handed down when words and deeds are consonant. If people don't see consistency—if, for instance, special favors are alleged around admissions, favorite students aren't disciplined for honor codes violations, misconduct by alumni contributors is overlooked, staff are maligned, colleagues are denigrated, responsibilities are not accepted—they conclude that the leader is, at best, not really serious, or, at worst, an outright hypocrite. If leaders do practice what they preach—and do so consistently—people are more willing to entrust them with their careers, their security, and their future.

This realization leads to a straightforward prescription for establishing credibility. DWYSYWD: Do What You Say You Will Do. This commonsense definition of credibility corresponds directly to the first of the Five Practices of Exemplary Leadership: Model the Way. To Model the Way and be credible in action, leaders must be clear about their beliefs; they must know what they stand for. That's the "say" part of DWYSYWD. Then they must put what they say into practice: they must act on their beliefs and "do." It is when leaders' words and deeds match up that people see them as credible. To gain and sustain the moral authority to lead, it's essential to Model the Way.

Because of this important connection between words and actions, we start our discussion of the Five Practices with a thorough examination of the principles and behaviors that bring Model the Way to life. There are other striking relationships between what leaders say they do when at their personal best and the attributes people look for and admire in their leaders. The leadership practice of Inspire a Shared Vision involves being forward-looking and inspiring. When leaders Challenge the Process, they enhance the perception that they're energetic and focused on future possibilities. Leaders who Enable Others to Act understand that their honesty fostered others' trust in them. Likewise, leaders who recognize and celebrate significant accomplishments—who Encourage the Heart—increase their constituents' understanding of the commitment to the vision and values. When leaders demonstrate capacity in all of the Five Practices, they show others they have the competence to get extraordinary things done. In the chapters that follow, we'll introduce you to some college and university leaders, people who lead from a wide range of positions, and who live the practices every day. These are the people who are getting extraordinary things done on campus.

2

Model the Way

THE FIRST THING LES COCHRAN DID after assuming his position as university president at Youngstown State University (YSU) was to purchase an abandoned building on the edge of campus and spend his free weekends working with construction crews to transform it into a residence for his family. While it's not unusual for college presidents to live near their campuses, Les's determination to do so attracted a great deal of attention and set the tone for his presidency.

To many observers, Les was literally putting his life on the line, for the once-lovely neighborhoods surrounding YSU had surrendered to increasingly aggressive gangs and escalating drug-related crime following the collapse of Youngstown's steel mill–dependent economy in the early 1980s. Les started the process of reclaiming YSU from the fear, hopelessness, apathy, and mistrust that paralyzed both it and the surrounding community. In doing so, he made it apparent that he was unquestionably dedicated to being an active participant "in making the world a better place to be." His message was clear: "We're responsible, both individually and collectively, for the fate of this community." Thus when he coined the slogan "Together we can make a difference"—his philosophy of individual contribution to community involvement—people knew he believed deeply in what he was saying. By buying and refurbishing a home in a decaying area he was determined to reclaim for YSU, Les "talked the talk" and "walked the talk."

Leaders, like Les, understand that they have to comprehend fully the values, beliefs, and assumptions that drive them. They have to freely and honestly choose the principles they will use to guide their actions. Before they can clearly communicate their message, they must be clear about the message they want to deliver. And before you can do what you say, you must be sure that you *mean* what you say.

What's required is being able to genuinely express your self. The words themselves aren't enough, no matter how noble. You must authentically communicate your beliefs in ways that uniquely represent who you are. You must interpret the lyrics and shape them into your own singular presentation so that others recognize that you're the one who's speaking and not someone else. "Above all else, academic deans—and all leaders—must come to terms with themselves," explains Deryl Leaming, himself a former dean and author of several books on academic leadership. He says, "They must understand their own inclinations and motivations and be comfortable with who they are" (Leaming, 2002, p. 438).

CLARIFY YOUR VALUES

What links the historical leaders people most admire *and* those whom they could imagine following willingly? Strong beliefs about matters of principle. The leaders most often named all have (or had, if they have died) unwavering commitment to a clear set of values. They all are, or were, passionate about their causes. They are comfortable with who they are and are not lacking in either self-knowledge or self-assurance. The lesson is unmistakable: to become a leader people would willingly follow requires being a person of principle. "The simple truth is that we cannot be leaders," Deryl explains, "unless others look up to and want to follow us, and the likelihood of that happening when we are insecure in who we are is remote" (Leaming, 2002, p. 438).

People expect their leaders to speak out on matters of values and conscience. But how can you speak out if you don't know what is important to you, what it is that you care deeply about? To earn and sustain personal credibility, you must be able to clearly articulate your deeply held beliefs. To speak effectively, it's essential to find your own true voice.

Lillas Brown had a successful career as a corporate human resource development manager at Federated Cooperatives Ltd., a large retailer and wholesaler. And she was looking for a way to have an expanded role in working with people in a different setting. "I wanted to make a difference," says Lillas, "in the lives of leaders and their constituents in the educational workplace." She was recruited to be the director of Business and Leadership Programs, a start-up operation in the University of Saskatchewan's Extension Division.

As she explained, "Like any new leader, I had to earn credibility. In any organization, credibility building is a process that takes time, hard work, devotion, and patience." But coming in as an outsider to higher education can be especially trying. There's skepticism about your intentions and the transferability of your competencies. This was even more true in Lillas's case, because one of the projects she initially took on was a leadership development program for department chairs. Imagine the rumblings: "How can someone from retailing possibly help develop the skills of those in academia?"

"In the early years," Lillas says, "some naysayers scoffed at my work, saying, 'You're talking about business and this is a university,' or 'You can't herd cats,' or 'Watch the fluff,' and so on. Painful as some of this was at the time, it not only contributed to my challenge, but it caused me to persevere. . . . It reinforced my intent to contribute to a more encouraging and nurturing culture than what I was experiencing." It made her even more mindful of the importance of delivering feedback "in a spirit that is useful and respectful."

Throughout this process Lillas turned to a simple method to aid her in staying the course. Every day she used personal journal writing for reflection and contemplation. "I use my journal to dialogue with the small still voice within," she says. "Every evening I ask, 'What have I done today that demonstrates this value that is near and dear to me? What have I done inadvertently to demonstrate this is not a value for me? What do I need to do more of to more fully express my values?'" By daily clarifying and reaffirming her values, Lillas was able to strengthen her resolve to contribute.

Lillas well understands that "a leader, just like any student, must want to engage in personal development." She has helped spark that desire on her campus: "We are developing a critical mass of chairs who are embracing leadership development and integrating it into our university culture." She has "seen a new department chair become an advisory committee member, serve his five years as chair, and then become the dean. That dean enthusiastically encourages his chairs to attend the leadership program and has recently encouraged a student leadership initiative in his College Student Association."

As Lillas's story illustrates, values are guides. They supply us with a moral compass by which to navigate the course of our daily lives. Clarity of values is essential to knowing which way, for each of us, is north, south, east, and west. The clearer we are, the easier it is to stay on the path we've chosen. This kind of guidance is especially needed in difficult and uncertain times. When there are daily challenges that can throw you off course, it's crucial that you have some signposts that tell you where you are.

Values also serve as guides to action. They inform our decisions as to what to do and what not to do; when to say yes, or no, and really understand *why* we mean it. If you believe, for instance, that collaborative discussion and even "heated debate" can stimulate thinking and creativity, then you should know what to do if people with differing views keep getting cut off when they offer up a fresh idea. If you value collaboration over individualistic achievement, then you'll know what to do when your most experienced career center counselor skips team meetings and refuses to share information with colleagues. If you value independence and initiative over conformity and obedience, you'll be more likely to challenge a policy when you think it's wrong.

EXPLORE YOUR INNER TERRITORY

When discussing a list of most admired leaders, our conversation went something like this:

Jim: I think leadership begins with discontent.
Barry: That's too dismal a view for me. I think leadership begins with caring.
Jim: Okay, then, let's look up caring in the dictionary.

We grabbed one off the shelf and opened it to *care*. The first meaning: "suffering of mind: GRIEF." There it was. Suffering and caring, discontent and concern, all come from one source. Deep within us all there is something we hold dear, something we'll fight hard to secure and celebrate joyfully when we achieve it.

In time, we realized that what we're both saying is *that leadership begins with something that grabs hold of you and won't let go.* There is something that isn't working, and you care enough to do something. Finding your voice requires exploring your inner territory. You have to take a journey into those places in your heart and soul where you bury your treasures, so that you can carefully examine them and eventually bring them out for display.

You *must* know what you care about. Why? Because you can only be authentic when leading others according to the principles that matter most to you. Otherwise you're just putting on an act. If you don't care, how can you expect others to do so? If you don't burn with desire to be true to something you hold passionately, how can you expect that commitment from others? And until you get close enough to the flame to feel the heat, how can you know the source?

It was questions such as these that California State University, Northridge, Professor Alan Glassman had to explore when he accepted his president's request to provide leadership to the institution's first strategic planning process. The process grew out of devastating damages (estimated at $350 million) from the Northridge earthquake. Several "highly paid and well-credentialed" external consultants had already been fired. Why then did Alan, who had been a faculty member for twenty-four years, take it on? As he explained, "I felt that I wanted to give something back to a campus that had supported me very well during my career." It was also a chance for him to participate and see firsthand the creation and development of a high involvement process for organizational change. As he said, "This experience was a test of both my belief systems and how well I could model my expectations of others." He saw the earthquake as an "unfreezing" experience and worked to create a high involvement model that offered people the opportunity to "create the future." As he told us, by appealing to people's desire to contribute, to do good, "we created space for volunteers to offer their services." And across campus, people confirmed one of Alan's deepest held values: given the chance, people will indeed do good.

As Alan discovered, becoming a credible leader requires learning how to express yourself in ways that are uniquely your own. You cannot lead through someone else's values, someone else's words. You cannot lead out of someone else's experience. You can only lead out of your own. Unless it's your style, your words, it's not you; it's an abstraction.

It's one thing to give voice to your words, it's another to give voice in tune and with a personal style. If you're not the genuine article, can you really expect others to respect you? People don't follow your technique. They follow you—your message and your embodiment of that message. To be a leader, you must confront this inner issue for yourself. You don't have to copy someone else, you don't have to read a script written by someone else, you don't have to wear someone else's style. Instead, you are free to choose what you want to express and the way you want to express it. In fact, we'd argue that you have a responsibility to your constituents to express yourself in a singular manner—in a way they would immediately recognize as yours.

BUILD AND AFFIRM SHARED VALUES

Clarity about personal values is an essential part of finding your voice. Yet leaders don't just stand up for some personal or idiosyncratic set of values. In the process of setting an example, leaders endeavor to lead their constituents from "what *I* believe" to "what *we* believe."

The underlying approach of the process that Alan Glassman led at Northridge was to foster cooperation between units on the campus, while respecting the distinctiveness of each unit. Doing so "required new ways of thinking about relationships and new ways of working together." As Alan explained, it had been commonplace to think of university-based strategic planning as the activity of a single entity (the university). So, "we changed the model, using the European Union as an analog—that is, many nations with different cultures (e.g., beliefs, values, norms) seeking a common good and recognizing inherent differences and the need for positive conflict resolution."

Discovering values that can be shared is the foundation for building productive and genuine working relationships. While credible leaders honor the diversity of their many constituencies, they also stress their common values. Leaders build on agreement. They don't try to get everyone to be in accord on everything—this goal is unrealistic, perhaps even impossible. Moreover, to achieve it would negate the very advantages of diversity. But to take a first step, and then a second, and then a third, people must have some common core of understanding. If disagreements over fundamental values continue, the result is intense conflict, false expectations, and diminished capacity.

Recognition of the values that faculty share, that the staff shares, that everyone on campus shares, serves to provide people with a common language. The research is clear that tremendous energy is generated when individual, group, and institutional values are aligned. Commitment, enthusiasm, and drive are intensified: people have reasons for caring about their work. When individuals are able to care about what they are doing, they are more effective and satisfied. They experience less stress and tension. Shared values are the internal compasses that enable people to act independently and interdependently—simultaneously.

The benefit to the campus from shared values is equally apparent: people are more loyal when they believe that their values and those of the institution are in synch. They can be more creative because they become immersed in what they are doing. The quality and accuracy of communication and the integrity of the decision-making process increase when people across the campus feel part of the same team.

Important as it is that leaders forthrightly articulate the principles for which they stand, what leaders say and do needs to be consistent with the aspirations of their constituents. When university administrators, at whatever level, advocate or speak out on values that aren't representative of the collective will, they are ineffective at mobilizing people to act as one. Leaders literally model the way by setting an example for all their constituents based on a shared understanding of what's expected. This means that they have gained consensus on a common cause and a common set of principles. This gives them legitimacy in building and affirming a community of shared values.

RENEW SHARED VALUES

Periodically taking the institution's pulse in regard to the clarity and consensus of its values is well worthwhile. It renews commitment. It engages the entire campus in discussing values (such as diversity, service learning, program assessment) to ensure that they are inclusive of an ever-changing constituency. Once people are clear about the leader's values, about their own values, and about shared values, they know what's expected of them; they can handle higher levels of uncertainty and ambiguity, and they can better deal with any conflicting demands between work and their personal lives.

But questions such as "What are our basic principles?" and "What do we believe in?" are far from simple. Even with commonly identified values, there may be little agreement on the meaning of values. At Santa Clara University, not an academic year goes by without everyone, or at least some significant portion of the campus, invested in discussions about core institutional values, such as "educating for competence, conscience, and compassion" or determining what it means to be a "Jesuit, Catholic" university. Leaders must engage their constituents in conversations about values issues. A common understanding of values comes about through that dialogue; it emerges from a *process,* not a pronouncement. After all, if there's no agreement about values, then what exactly is the leader—and everyone else—going to model?

For values to be truly shared, they must be more than campus or program advertising slogans. They must be deeply supported and broadly endorsed beliefs about what's important to the people who hold them. Faculty and staff must be able not only to enumerate the values but provide relatively common interpretations of how those values are put into practice. They must know how the values influence the way they teach, provide services to students and alumni, issues they address, ceremonies they hold, and so on, as well as feel that these values contribute directly to making their college or university unique and distinctive.

Shared values emerge from listening, appreciating, building consensus, and practicing conflict resolution. For people on campus and within various departments and programs to understand the values and come to agree with them, they must participate in the process. A unified voice on values results from discovery and dialogue: *unity is forged, not forced.* Leaders must provide a chance for individuals to engage in a discussion of what the values mean and how their personal beliefs and behaviors are influenced by what the institution stands for. Leaders must also be prepared to discuss values and expectations in the recruitment, selection, and orientation of new faculty and staff members. Better to explore early the fit between person and organization than to have people find out late some sleepless night that they're in violent disagreement over matters of principle.

LEAD BY EXAMPLE

Leaders *enact* the meaning of the organization in every decision they make and in every step they take toward the future they envision. Leaders understand that they bring shared values to life in a variety of settings—in everyday department meetings; one-on-one conferences; telephone calls; faculty and staff council sessions; and visits with alumni, vendors, suppliers, and community members.

As Alan explained to us, he and the president of Northridge "decided early on that we had to model the value of civil discourse. Since we did see several issues differently, we agreed that we should disagree openly, yet constructively, at public meetings. It was not unusual for her to say, 'Our consultant recommends . . . but I think we should . . .' This allowed me to maintain my faculty perspective and be seen by the campus as an 'honest broker.' As important, it was real evidence that civil discourse and open discussion were highly valued."

The essential repertoire of leaders in setting an example for others includes how they spend their time, how they react to critical incidents, the stories they tell, and the language and questions they choose. Application of these tools of leadership isn't haphazard. Although serendipity may play a role, leaders are constantly on the lookout for ways to establish themselves as leaders.

Modeling the way via these tools may appear rather basic and obvious. But it's all in the attention, the doing: it's their conscious application that challenges aspiring leaders and their lack of execution that fosters cynicism in constituents. What each affords is the opportunity to make visible and tangible to others a conscious commitment to a shared way of being.

Spend Time and Pay Attention

How you spend your time is the single clearest indicator, especially to other people, about what's important to you. If you say your top priority is faculty, students, staff, or alumni, then how much of your daily time do you spend with them? When Jeanne O'Laughlin, O.P., was president at Barry University, her vision was to create a caring environment on campus; to back that up, she would routinely stop and talk with every student she met as she walked across campus. Leaders make a conscious connection between how they allocate their time or schedule their calendars and what they consider to be their priorities and key values.

Setting an example often means arriving early, staying late, and being there to show you care. It's about being the first to do something that everyone should value. Career Services Director Andy Ceperley demonstrates by his own demeanor and behavior how people ought to treat one another rather than trying to simply tell them. Faculty members who arrive early to their classes and linger afterward to answer questions and chat with students successfully communicate their own and their institution's commitment to caring about students. The first day on the job found Nan Keohane of Wellesley College pedaling to work on an old bicycle and chaining it to the sign that said "President's Car"—another quite simple statement about values. Father Pat Murphy at DePaul University put it this way: "Effective college leaders are teachers, too. The best of them teach values" (Murphy, 1991, p. 2).

Turn Critical Incidents into Teachable Moments

Choosing to spend time on what's important is essential to sending the signal that you're serious about an issue. Yet even the most disciplined leaders can't stop the intrusion of the unexpected and the serendipitous.

There are constant interruptions, brief interactions, and extraordinary variety in the everyday life of the college campus. Critical incidents—chance occurrences, particularly at a time of stress and challenge—offer significant moments of learning for leaders and constituents. Critical incidents—whatever the locale—present opportunities for leaders to teach important lessons about appropriate norms of behavior.

Jim Lyons, former dean of students at Stanford University, was always on the lookout for critical incidents that he called, for the campus, "teachable moments." These were the times that something unexpected happened, usually negative (but not always), and campus administrators had a leadership choice to make about how they wanted to frame and respond to the incident. When a violation of the university's honor code occurs (as it will inevitably), the incident can be narrowly focused on dealing with those students who were caught cheating. Alternatively, the incident can be more broadly focused to bring the entire campus community—student body, faculty, and staff—into a discussion of what it means to have, and live by, an honor code. What does it mean to be responsible not just for one's self but to be responsible for how others behave? Incidents will happen, and the question for leaders is what do they want to teach as a consequence?

For example, much of the movement in university housing departments and programs has shifted over the years from focusing on making certain that people don't break the rules to examining ways to encourage people to follow the rules, often rules that the residents themselves have determined are the "shared values" by which they want to live as a community.

Critical incidents are those events in leaders' lives that offer the chance to improvise while still staying true to the script. Although they can't be explicitly planned, it's useful to keep in mind that the way you handle these incidents—how you link actions and decisions to shared values—says volumes about what's important.

Tell Stories to Teach Virtues

Critical incidents are often the most dramatic sources of moral lessons about what we should and should not value, about how we should and should not behave. They become stories that are passed down, whether around the classrooms, residence halls, among faculty and staff as well as students, and even from generation to generation.

While the leader's message is important, and how it is framed is critical, the process by which it is communicated is just as significant. Several people can present the same basic message and receive entirely different responses from their audience. How we educate and how our messages are communicated have much to do with whether what we say will be remembered, endorsed, and followed.

A leader's words "often assume their greatest impact as symbols rather than as literal meanings" (Conger, 1991). This is especially true when words are used to tell a story. Stories serve as a kind of mental map that helps people know, first, what is important (purpose and values) and, second, how things are done in a particular group or organization.

Judith Ramaley, former biology professor and college president, now with the National Science Foundation, tells aspiring leaders to have members of their college community tell them about the good things that are happening and what they think is happening that especially contributes to the quality of the institution in quiet, even subtle, ways. Armed with this material, she says, "you can be a storyteller. . .and your stories will help create meaning and direction for the institution" (Ramaley, 2002).

When a leader is trying to communicate the values of an organization, what would have more of an impact on you? A policy statement that says "Thou shalt establish personal relationships with alumni," or a story told about the dean attending the Alumni Association's monthly TGIFs? If you said the story, your answer jibes with the data. In fact, information is more quickly and accurately remembered when it is first presented in the form of an example or story, especially compared to facts, figures, and formal policy pronouncements (Denning, 2001; Ready, 2002).

What's one of the best examples of storytelling used to shape behaviors and influence cultural norms and personal values? The Bible. Stories are far better able to accomplish the objectives of teaching, mobilizing, and motivating than bullet points on an overhead. Well-told stories reach inside us and pull us along. They give us the sense of being there and of learning what is really important about the experience.

Choose Words and Questions Deliberately

Harvard professor Shoshana Zuboff has observed that we are "prisoners" of our organizational vocabulary (Zuboff, 1988, p. 394). If you disagree, try talking about your college or university for even a day without using the words *employee, manager, boss, supervisor, staff, subordinate,* or *hierarchy*. We've all come to accept certain words we use as the reality of organizational life. Those words can trap us into a particular way of thinking about our roles and relationships.

Leaders understand the power of words and are attentive to language. The words we choose to use are metaphors for concepts that define attitudes and behaviors, structures and systems. Our words evoke images of what we hope to create and how we expect people to behave. Too often on college campuses some people hold tightly to designations that set them apart (and preferably above) others. Such distinctions make it challenging to find common ground. Consider the simple shift in language and meaning when the vernacular "extracurricular"—to describe those activities on campus directed by the student affairs divisions—was dropped in favor of "cocurricular" to recognize the holistic notion of the educational and learning process on campus. The shift in thinking on college campuses from building "dormitories" to creating "residential learning communities" is another effort in this same direction. With this shift in designation (language) comes a necessary shift in understanding the role that many staff members, along with the faculty, play in the education of young men and women while they are on campus.

Questions, too, are quite powerful in focusing attention. Just like a faculty member in a classroom, when leaders ask questions, they send people on mental journeys—"quests"—in search of answers. The questions that leaders ask send messages about what's of most importance to them and point to the focus of their department or program. Questions constitute one more measure of how serious we are about our espoused beliefs; they indicate which values should be attended to and how much energy should be devoted to them.

A key leadership insight for Jackie Schmidt-Posner, when she was the adviser for a large student-run conference ("You Can Make a Difference") at Stanford University, was the importance of raising questions. The questions she asked "brought the student coordinators back to focus on the vision and purpose of the project. Once they had their eye on the ball, they could develop the necessary strategies." Jackie realized that a significant part of her role was often "to focus the group through asking the tough questions." Questions frame the issue and set the agenda.

DEVELOP COMPETENCE

Words alone do not make a leader credible. Having a clear and authentic message is a necessary first step, yet the ability to consistently deliver the message and act on it requires a high level of skill. Before you can do the right things, you have to know how to do them. You cannot do what you don't know how to do, no matter how moral or noble the purpose and regardless of whether others affirm the direction.

To commit to doing something without the capacity to perform it is either disingenuous or stupid. There's nothing courageous about boldly saying you'll successfully launch a new curriculum or turn around a residential learning community if you have neither the skills nor the resources to do it. Leaders must be aware of the degree to which they actually have the capabilities to do what they say. And if they lack the competence they must dedicate themselves to continuously learning and improving.

This is something Jackie kept firmly in mind in working with the students at Stanford. As she said, "I shared my own learnings—including mistakes—with the students and I was willing to change direction based on new information." She made sure she was part of the learning community and, rather than framing herself as an expert, acknowledged areas (student culture and schedules, as just two examples) in which the students clearly knew more and could teach her.

Acquiring competence is all about being genuine. People who boast of being able to perform a task or achieve a goal, or who make exaggerated claims of possessing noble attributes or desirable material goods, are called phonies and fakes and are seldom followed for very long. Your value as a leader is determined by your guiding beliefs—and by your ability to act on them. To be genuine requires you to honestly and continuously assess your existing abilities and be willing to learn new ones. Keep in mind that, left untended, everyone's skills and abilities, like any other asset, deteriorate over time. And it should come as no surprise to anyone on a college campus that learning takes time and conscious attention. If leaders expect others to do things that they have never done before, which is the basis for any improvement or innovative effort, then creating a climate where people can learn and not be afraid to admit that there are areas where they can learn is essential. Such a climate occurs only in those situations where leaders are also willing to Model the Way by participating in the learning process themselves.

MODELING THE WAY

Each and every one of us earns credibility as a leader on a daily basis. To be a leader, you have to Model the Way for others by demonstrating intense commitment to your beliefs with each and every action. Doing so begins by finding your voice—by clarifying your values and by expressing yourself in unique ways.

By finding your voice you take the first step along the endless journey to becoming a credible leader. By constantly asking yourself what value you bring to your constituents you'll always stay at the leading edge. Beyond clarifying your personal values is the building, affirming, and renewing of values that leaders and their constituents alike can embrace.

Setting the example is essentially the "doing" part of what you "say" you will do. Walking the talk is the first test of the leader's credibility. Leaders are measured by the con-

MODEL THE WAY

- Clarify your values
- Explore your inner territory
- Build and affirm shared values
- Renew shared values
- Lead by example
- Spend time and pay attention
- Turn critical incidents into teachable moments
- Tell stories to teach virtues
- Choose words and questions deliberately
- Develop competence

sistency of their deeds and words. Leaders show up, pay attention, and participate directly in the process of getting extraordinary things done. Leaders take every opportunity to show others by their own example that they're deeply committed to the values and aspirations they espouse. Leading by example is how leaders make visions and values tangible. It's how they provide the *evidence* that they're personally committed and competent.

3

Inspire a Shared Vision

WHEN JOAN CARTER TOOK OVER as general manager and executive chef of the Faculty Club at Santa Clara University, both membership and sales had been seriously declining for several years. The remaining customers were unhappy, the restaurant's balance sheet was "scary," and the staff was divided into factions.

Joan took all this in, and what she saw was a dusty diamond. "I saw a beautiful and historic building full of mission-era flavor and character that should be, could be, would be *the* place on campus." In her mind's eye, she saw the club bustling. She saw professors and university staff chatting on the lovely enclosed patio and enjoying high-quality, appealing, yet inexpensive meals. She smiled as she envisioned the club assisting alumni in planning wonderful, personal, and professionally catered wedding receptions and anniversary celebrations.

Joan could see a happy staff whose primary concern was customer satisfaction, a kitchen that produced a product far superior to "banquet food," and a catering staff that did whatever it took to make an event exceptional. She wasn't quite sure how the club had deteriorated to the extent it had, but that really didn't matter. She decided to ignore the quick fix and set out to teach everyone how unique and wonderful the club could be.

Over the next two years, as she talked with customers and worked with her staff, she instilled a vision of the club as a restaurant that celebrated good food and good company. As food and service quality began to improve, smiles became more prevalent among customers and staff, and sales began to rise: 20 percent the first year and 30 percent again the next. When a top financial manager of the university asked how she had turned the finances around so quickly and dramatically, Joan responded, "You can't turn around numbers. The balance sheet is just a reflection of what's happening here, every day, in the restaurant. I just helped the staff realize what we're really all about. It was always here," she said, "only perhaps a little dusty, a little ignored, and a little unloved. I just helped them see it."

The leaders we interviewed, like Joan, echo the perspective that bringing meaning to life in the present by focusing on making life better in the long run is essential in getting extraordinary things done. All enterprises or projects, big or small, begin in the mind's eye; they begin with imagination and with the belief that what's merely an image can one day be made real.

HAVE A VISION

No matter what term is used—whether *purpose, mission, legacy, dream, goal, calling,* or *personal agenda*—the intent is the same: leaders want to do something significant, accomplishing something that no one else has yet achieved. What that something is—the sense of meaning and purpose—has to come from within. That's why, just as we said about values, you must first clarify your own visions of the future before you can expect to enlist others in a shared vision. To create a climate of meaningfulness, first you must personally believe in something yourself. Before you can inspire others, you have to be inspired yourself. Your passion for something is an indication of what you find worthy in and of itself. It's a clue to what you find *intrinsically* rewarding.

You can't impose a vision on others. It has to be something that has meaning to them, not just to you. Leaders must foster conditions under which people will do things because they want to, not because they have to. One of *the* most important practices of leadership is giving life and work a sense of meaning and purpose by offering an exciting vision. Leaders create environments where departmental (institutional) visions and personal values intersect.

In this digital age, people often ask: "How can I have a vision of what's going to happen on this campus, in this state, yet alone in higher education, five or ten or even two years from now, when I don't even know what's going to happen next week or even next term?" Look at it this way: Imagine you're driving along the Pacific Coast Highway heading south from San Francisco on a bright, sunny day. The hills are on your left; the ocean, on your right. On some curves, the cliffs plunge several hundred feet to the water. You can see for miles and miles.

You're cruising along at the speed limit, tunes blaring, top down, wind in your hair, and not a care in the world. Suddenly, without warning, you come around a bend in the road and there's a blanket of fog as thick as you've ever seen it. What do you do? We've asked this question many, many times and we get the same answers: I slow way down, I turn my lights on, I grab the steering wheel with both hands, I tense up, I lean forward, and I turn the radio off so I can hear better. Then you go around the next curve in the road, the fog lifts, and it's clear again. What do you do? Relax, speed up, turn the lights off, turn the radio on, and enjoy the scenery.

This analogy illustrates the importance of clarity of vision, *especially* when you're going fast. How fast can you drive in the fog without risking your own or other people's lives? How comfortable are you riding in a car with someone else who drives fast in the fog? Are you able to go faster when it's foggy or when it's clear? It's obvious, isn't it? We're better able to go fast when our vision is clear. We're better able to anticipate the switchbacks and bumps in the road when we can see ahead, the farther the better.

DISCOVER YOUR THEME

Just knowing they're important doesn't make visions pop out of your head like bright light bulbs. When we ask people to tell us where their visions come from, they often have great difficulty describing the process. And when they do provide an answer, typically it's more about a feeling, a sense, a gut reaction, a hunch. When people first take on their roles as leaders—whether they're appointed or whether they volunteer—they often don't have a *clear* vision of the future.

At the beginning, what leaders on college campuses have is a *theme*. They have concerns, desires, hypotheses, propositions, arguments, hopes, and dreams—core concepts around which they organize their aspirations and actions. Leaders begin the process of envisioning the future by discovering their themes. Everything else leaders say about their vision is an elaboration, interpretation, and variation on that theme. Fortunately, there are ways to improve your ability to articulate your own themes and ultimately your visions of the future.

Finding your vision, like finding your voice, is a process of self-exploration and self-creation. It's an intuitive, emotional process. There's often no logic to it. What we've seen is that exemplary leaders have a passion for their departments and institutions, their causes, their programs, their students, their subject matter, their technologies, their communities—something other than their own fame and fortune. Leaders care about something much bigger than themselves and much bigger than all of us. Leaders care about making a difference by making the status quo better in some meaningful way.

If you don't care deeply for and about something and someone, then how can you expect others to feel any sense of conviction? How can you expect others to get jazzed if you're not energized and excited? How can you expect others to suffer through the long hours and hard work if you're not similarly committed?

We asked Kent Koth why he selected a particular project as his personal-best leadership experience. His answer speaks volumes about how in leading others we discover our passions: "This was the defining moment in my budding professional life. It was at this moment that I knew what I was born to do. I had found my place in the world."

When Kent was on the staff of Willamette University (Salem, Oregon) as Community Outreach Program Coordinator, he wanted to provide an educational and service opportunity for students to engage with issues and people with whom they were unfamiliar. He traveled to San Francisco with a group of students for the campus's first ever "alternative" spring break. This group slept on the floor of a San Francisco church and worked at local homeless shelters and with the AIDS Memorial Quilt. Each night they cooked dinner together and discussed the day's events as they ate. After dinner they gathered as a group to participate in team-building exercises, discuss social issues related to their service experiences, write in the group's journal, and prepare for the next day's work. His fondest wish for the project, Kent told us "was for students to return to campus with a new sense of passion and commitment to social justice. I hoped the trip would serve as the spark to ignite a lifelong exploration of commitment to others. I dreamed that these students would come away stronger, wiser, and more compassionate." Kent discovered his theme: "I possessed a passion for justice that motivated me to construct a project that would raise complicated ethical issues. Everyone is equal. Everyone has a gift to give. Everyone has something to learn. Love and justice can guide us to a new level of awareness."

EXPLORE YOUR PAST

What's the relevance of our past experience to envisioning the future? In one study, senior executives were asked to look ahead into their personal future—to "think of things that might (or will) happen to you in the future." In another part of the study, they were asked to look into their personal past—to "think of the things that have happened to you in the past." In each case, they were asked to list ten events and to date each event.

Divided randomly into two groups, one listed the past events first; the other group listed the future events first. The executives who listed their past events first had significantly longer future time horizons—over four years longer—than the executives who listed future events first. The two groups had similar past time horizons, both with a maximum of about twenty years.

The most plausible explanation for this result was: "We make sense of our world retrospectively, and all understanding originates in reflection and looking backward. We construct the future by some kind of extrapolation, in which the past is prologue, and the approach to the future is backward-looking" (El Sawy, 1983, p. VII-35).

This is precisely the feeling that one of our colleagues, Jack Ciechon, recently shared with us when we took him through this experience. He told us:

My earlier view, and an all too common one, of developing the "vision thing" is that by "gazing into the crystal ball" I might somehow intuit the shape of things to come. In practice this meant spending some time meditating or thinking on questions such as, "What should my goals for the organization [my group] be?" or "What is my vision statement for our group?" This approach was usually just a frustrating exercise. I attributed this to the relatively short time I would spend thinking about the issues and thought that if I just spent more time thinking about my vision, it would come.

It came as a great insight to me that a useful framework for posing the future vision question to myself was to consider my past. Using the past as a starting point for envisioning the future provides two strong reference points: it helps me identify the passions in my life and provides clarity to my values. It seems self-evident that my vision of the future should include my passions. I see now that "gazing in the crystal ball" lacked passion; it didn't involve me enough to care about the future.

Also I can clearly see how important my personal values are to developing and communicating a vision of the future. Trusting in my personal ethics and integrity provides the guidance needed to focus the energy for leadership that my passions provide.

As Jack learned to appreciate, when we gaze first into our past, we elongate our future. We also enrich our future and give it detail as we recall the richness of our past experiences. So, to be able to envision the possibilities in the distant future, look first into the past. When you do, you're likely to find that your central theme has been there for a long time.

In addition to identifying lifelong themes, there's another benefit to looking back before looking ahead: we can gain a greater appreciation for how long it can take to fulfill aspirations. We also realize that there are many, many avenues for us to pursue and that there may actually be no specific end in sight when it comes to aspirations.

None of this is to say that the past *is* our future. Adopting that extremely dangerous perspective would be like trying to drive to the future while looking only in the rearview mirror. With that point of view, we'd drive ourselves and our organizations right off a cliff. Avail yourself of the richest set of experiences possible. The broader your experiences and the more vast your network of connections, the longer your time horizons are likely to be.

IMMERSE YOURSELF

As you acquire experience, you acquire information about what happens, how things happen, and who makes things happen in an organization, a profession, on a campus, or with an industry. When you're presented with an unfamiliar problem, you consciously (or unconsciously) draw upon your experiences to help solve it. You select crucial information, make relevant comparisons, and integrate experience with the current situation. For the experienced leader, all of this may happen in a matter of seconds. But it's the years of direct contact with a variety of problems and situations that equip the leader with unique insight; listening, reading, feeling, and sensing—these experiences improve the leader's vision. Leaders develop an intuitive sense or gut feel for what is going to happen down the road—they can anticipate the future (Klein, 1998; Breen, 2000).

Jo-Anne Shibles speaks of a "gut reaction" that told her the Student Leadership Institute she was asked to develop at California State University, Fullerton, could be very successful. Jo-Anne, who was at the time activities coordinator within the Office of Student Life, believed from the start that she could pull the program off. She was excited by it and could visualize in some detail how the program would run. As she told us: "I could see students sitting in a class listening to a faculty member talk about ethical dilemmas. I could see small groups of students talking about how our different cultural backgrounds influence our leadership. I could see students being excited to get their certificates at our reception at the end of the program." From her gut feel—and lots of work—came a successful pilot program in which fifty students explored their leadership style and developed leadership skills. Now, more than ten years after it started, the project still makes Jo-Anne smile—and it continues on the campus, developing an ever-growing group of students.

Like Jo-Anne, many of the people we interviewed mentioned that the exercise of analyzing their personal-best leadership experiences was enlightening for them: by highlighting key lessons from the past, they were able to generate insightful road maps for leadership highways still to be explored. Direct experience with the organization, the industry, or the profession is critical. It's the knowledge gained from direct experience and active searching that, once stored in the subconscious, becomes the basis for leaders' intuition, insight, and vision.

Envisioning the future is a process that begins with a feeling or an inspiration that something is worth doing. Your vision of the future may be fuzzy, but at least you're focused on a meaningful theme. You believe that the present situation could be better than it is today; you act on your instincts and the vision gets a little clearer. You do something else that moves you; the vision gets a little clearer still. You pay attention to it, experience it, immerse yourself in it. Get the process started and, over time, you see more detail in your dream. It's an iterative process, one that eventually results in something that you can actually articulate.

FIND MEANING IN THE IDEAL

Visions are about hopes, aspirations, and themes. They're about our strong desire to achieve something great. They're ambitious. They're expressions of optimism. Can you imagine a leader enlisting others in a cause by saying, "I'd like you to join me in doing the ordinary better"? Not likely. Visions necessarily stretch us to imagine exciting possibilities, breakthrough programs, or revolutionary social change.

By focusing on the ideal we also gain a sense of meaning and purpose from what we undertake. It's one thing to go on an adventure just for the fun of it; it's another to do it because it feeds the soul. The visions of leaders are about making a difference in the world, about having an impact. Of course, the two aren't mutually exclusive; we should always have fun pursuing our dreams.

"We started something from nothing." This is how Dennis Dow described his vision of a counseling center at Notre Dame de Namur University (Belmont, California), and he "never doubted that this center, started in 1982, would continue to evolve." Indeed, even as Dennis continued to add new services and brought new capabilities to the center (and campus community), he's still looking forward, an attitude captured by the Robert Louis Stevenson quote on the center's brochure: "To travel hopefully is better than to have arrived."

All the personal-best cases we collected were, like Dennis's, about possibilities for the future. They were about improving on the existing situation or creating an entirely new state of existence. The leaders were dissatisfied with the status quo and believed that something better was attainable. They represent the choice of an ideal.

TAKE PRIDE IN BEING UNIQUE

Visions communicate what makes us singular and unequaled; they set us apart from everyone else. There's no advantage in working for an institution that does exactly the same thing as the one across town. For students, faculty, staff, or alumni to want to sign up with us, they have to first understand how we're truly distinctive, how we stand out from the crowd. Uniqueness fosters pride. It boosts the self-respect and self-esteem of everyone associated with the organization. The more proud we are of the college where we work, the students and alumni we "produce," or the people with whom we interact, the more loyal we're likely to be.

Uniqueness also enables smaller units within large organizations to have their own vision while still being encompassed by the collective vision. Although every unit within a college must be aligned with the overall organizational vision, it can express its distinctive purpose within the larger whole. Every function and every department can differentiate itself by finding its most distinctive qualities. Each can be proud of its ideal and unique image of its future as it works toward the common future of the larger organization.

CREATE IMAGES OF THE FUTURE

A beacon of light cutting through the fog. It's an image you can picture in your mind. In fact, leaders often talk about future issues in terms of foresight, focus, forecasts, future scenarios, points of view, and perspectives. Visual references, all. In our workshops and classes we often illustrate the power of images with this simple exercise. We ask people to think about the city of Paris, France, and to shout out the first thing that comes to mind. The replies—the Eiffel Tower, the Arc de Triomphe, the Seine, Notre Dame, good food, wine, romance—are all images of real places and real sensations. No one calls out the square kilometers, population, or gross domestic product of Paris. The same would be true for your college or university campus. Why? Human memory is stored in images and sensory impressions, not in numbers. We recall images of reality, not abstractions from reality.

When we invent the future, we need to get a mental picture of what things will be like long before we begin the journey. Images are our windows on the world of tomorrow. When talking about going to places we've never been we imagine what they'd look like.

In spreading word of the Student Leadership Institute across the campus at California State University, Fullerton, Jo-Anne Shibles helped others imagine it. She emphasized "that the program had not been done before." As she told students being recruited for the pilot project, "This is new. It is going to be great—and you are part of making it great. Imagine being able to learn how to build a team within your club, deal with someone who is not doing their job, explore how to run an effective meeting." Jo-Anne created real images of the concrete skills that students would gain by being involved. She explained how they could do all this in a few hours a week, in time between classes. By spending time one-on-one and with small groups, she sold the vision and made it real.

Just as Jo-Anne did, leaders animate the vision and make manifest the purpose so that others can see it, hear it, taste it, touch it, feel it. Leaders make full use of the power of language in communicating a shared identity and giving life to visions. Successful leaders use metaphors and other figures of speech; they make conscious use of metaphorical expressions to give vividness and tangibility to abstract ideas. Leaders draw word pictures, give examples, tell stories, and relate anecdotes. Leaders find ways of giving expression to their hopes for the future. In making the intangible vision tangible, leaders ignite constituents' flames of passion. Leaders bring the vision to life.

DEVELOP A SHARED SENSE OF DESTINY

People frequently talked about the need to get buy-in on the vision in their personal-best leadership cases. They explained how they had to communicate the purpose and build support for the direction. It's not enough for a leader to have a vision—the members of the department must understand, accept, and commit to the vision. When they do, the department and institution's ability to change and reach its potential soars.

Simply put, you have to teach others your vision. Teaching a vision—and confirming that the vision is shared—is a process of engaging constituents in conversations about their lives, about their own hopes and dreams. Leadership isn't about imposing the leader's solo dream; it's about developing a *shared* sense of destiny. It's about enrolling others so that they can see how their own interests and aspirations are aligned with the vision and can thereby become mobilized to commit their individual energies to its realization. A vision is *inclusive* of constituents' aspirations.

LISTEN DEEPLY

Identifying who your constituents are and finding out what their common aspirations are is one of the first required steps that leaders take in enlisting others. No matter how grand the dream of an individual visionary, if others don't see in it the possibility of realizing their own hopes and desires, they won't follow. Leaders must show others how they, too, will be served by the long-term vision of the future, how their specific needs can be satisfied.

Leaders find themselves listening deeply so as to sense the purpose in others. By knowing their constituents, by listening to them, and by soliciting their advice, leaders are able to give voice to constituents' feelings. They're able to stand before others and say with assurance, "Here's what I heard you say that you want for yourselves. Here's how your own needs and interests will be served by enlisting in a common cause." In a sense, leaders hold up a mirror and reflect back to their constituents what they say they most desire. When the constituents see that reflection, they recognize it and are immediately attracted to it.

Understanding leadership as a reciprocal relationship puts listening in its proper perspective. Leaders know that they can't do it alone. Leaders know that they don't have to have all the ideas or know all of the answers. The seeds of any vision arise not from crystal-ball-gazing in the upper levels of the campus administration but from images passed on from graduates, colleagues, and even frontline personnel. The best leaders are often the best followers.

There are many reasons why college presidents, including University of Southern California's Stephen Sample and University of Oregon's Dave Frohnmayer, still teach classes. The big ones are to be in direct contact with entering students, talking with them directly without any intervening administrative filters. It brings them firsthand, current experiences of being a teacher on their campus. For example, it allows them to know, from their own personal encounters, just how supportive various services are to faculty, students, and staff.

Sensitivity to others is no trivial skill; rather, it is a truly precious human ability. But it isn't *complex:* it requires receptiveness to other people and a willingness to listen. It means being delicately aware of the attitudes and feelings of others and the nuances of their communication.

To truly hear what constituents want—what they desperately hope to make you understand, appreciate, and include within the vision—requires periodically suspending regular activities and spending time listening to others. This means getting out of your office and spending time with other faculty and staff colleagues in *their* offices, having coffee, breakfast, lunch, afternoon breaks, or some unstructured time with constituent groups and finding out what's going on with them and what they are hoping to achieve from their relationship with you.

DISCOVER A COMMON PURPOSE

Have you asked people why they stay? More likely, and especially if staffing is part of your responsibilities on campus, you worry about turnover and retention rates and why people leave. But think about the vast majority of those who stay. Why do they stay? Why do you? The most important reason people give is that they find the work they are doing to be challenging, meaningful, and purposeful (Kaye and Jordon-Evans, 1999). Academic institutions, on either the faculty or staff side, have an advantage over many other types of organizations in that our members generally start out with a shared commitment to learning and personal (professional) development. Listening with sensitivity to the aspirations of others reveals that there are common values that link everyone on campus together: a chance to be tested, to make it on one's own; a chance to take part in a social experiment; a chance to do something well; a chance to do something good; and a chance to change the way things are (Berlew, 1974; Berlew, personal communication, November 14, 1994; Diamond, 2002). Aren't these the essence of what most leadership challenges, as well as opportunities, are all about?

What people want from their workplace has not changed very dramatically through the years despite economic upturns and downturns. Regardless of profession, industry, or location, people rank "interesting work" well above "high income." And quality of leadership ("working for a leader with vision and values") is even more motivating than dollars. The most frequently mentioned measure of success in worklife? Does it surprise you to learn that "personal satisfaction for doing a good job" is cited between three and four times as often as "getting ahead" or "making a good living"? ("The Retention Dilemma," 2001; Lucas, 2000).

Universities have seldom been a place where people have gone to work in order to maximize their financial gains. Hence there's rich opportunity for campus leaders to appeal to much more than material rewards. Great leaders create meaning. The values and interests of freedom, self-actualization, learning, community, excellence, justice, service, and social responsibility truly attract people to a common cause. Shared visions, notes MIT professor Peter Senge, are "a force in people's hearts, a force of impressive power" (Senge, 1990, p. 206).

There is a deep human yearning to make a difference. We want to know that we've done something on this earth, that there's a purpose to our existence. Work can provide that purpose, and increasingly work is where men and women seek it. Work has become a place where people pursue meaning and identity (Palmer, 2000). The best university-based leaders are able to bring out and make use of this human longing by communicating the meaning and significance of the college's work so that people understand their own important role in creating it. When leaders clearly communicate a shared vision of an organization, they ennoble those who work on its behalf. They elevate the human spirit.

PRACTICE POSITIVE COMMUNICATION

We want leaders with enthusiasm, with a bounce in their step, with a positive attitude. This conveys that we'll be part of an invigorating journey. We follow people with a can-do attitude, not those cynics who give twenty-five reasons why something can't be done or who don't make us feel good about ourselves or what we're doing.

The leaders people most admire are electric, vigorous, active, full of life. We're reminded of our colleague Randi DuBois, one of the founders of Pro-Action, who gets people to stretch themselves by engaging in challenging physical tasks. Typically, her clients are nervous, even a bit scared at first. But people of all ages, all sizes, and all physical abilities have successfully completed the Pro-Action outdoor challenge courses. How does Randi succeed in leading these people? Her secret is very simple: she's always positive that people can do the course, and she never says never. She conveys very clearly that people have the power within themselves to accomplish whatever they desire. (Both authors know this from personal experience. We've been forty feet above the ground leaping off a small platform for an iron ring while Randi cheered us on.)

BE EXPRESSIVE

In explaining why particular leaders have a magnetic effect, people often describe them as charismatic. But *charisma* has become such an overused and misused term that it's almost useless as a descriptor of leaders. "In the popular media," notes leadership scholar Bernard Bass, "charisma has come to mean anything ranging from chutzpah to Pied Piperism, from celebrity to superman status. It has become an overworked cliché for strong, attractive, and inspiring personality" (Bass, 1985, p. 35).

Social scientists have attempted to investigate this elusive quality in terms of observable behavior (Goleman, McKee, and Boyatzis, 2002; Conger, 1998). What they've found is that people who are perceived to be charismatic are simply more animated than others. They smile more, speak faster, pronounce words more clearly, and move their heads and bodies more often. They are also more likely to reach out and touch or make some physical contact with others during greetings. What we call *charisma*, then, can better be understood as expressiveness.

People underestimate themselves in this area: we've found that people's common perception of themselves as uninspiring is in sharp contrast to their performance when talking about their personal-best leadership cases or about their ideal futures. When relating hopes, dreams, and successes, people are almost always emotionally expressive. Expressiveness comes naturally when talking about deep desires for the future. People lean forward in their chairs, they move their arms about, their eyes light up, their voices sing with emotion, and they smile. They are enthusiastic, articulate, optimistic, and uplifting. In short, people *are* inspiring! Most of us just have to be willing to share the enthusiasm we have with others, rather than locking it away and assuming that expressiveness is not "professional." Nonsense! Leaders who make a difference on campus lead from the heart.

INSPIRING A SHARED VISION

Visions give focus to human energy. This enables each person concerned with the department, program, or institution to see more clearly what's ahead of them and what the future will look like when everyone has added their piece. With this in mind, they can contribute to the whole, efficiently and with confidence.

Leaders in our studies share the characteristic of being forward-looking, of being concerned not just about today's problems but also about tomorrow's possibilities. They're able to envision the future, to gaze across the horizon of time and imagine the greater opportunities to come. They see something out ahead, vague as it might appear from a distance, and they imagine that extraordinary feats are possible and that the ordinary could be transformed into something noble.

Leaders breathe life into visions. They enlist others by communicating their hopes and dreams so that others clearly understand and accept them as their own. Leaders know what motivates their constituents. They show others how their values and interests will be served by a particular long-term vision of the future. Above all, they're convinced of the value of that vision, and express that genuine belief with others in ways that generate enthusiasm and excitement for the common vision.

INSPIRE A SHARED VISION

- Have a vision
- Discover your theme
- Explore your past
- Immerse yourself
- Find meaning in the ideal
- Take pride in being unique
- Create images of the future
- Develop a shared sense of destiny
- Listen deeply
- Discover a common purpose
- Practice positive communication
- Be expressive

4

Challenge the Process

ENO TAINI AND RANDI DUBOIS KNOW what it takes for people to grow and develop, to make mistakes, learn, and experience the small wins that sustain commitment. Their organization, Pro-Action, sponsors programs in which participants learn through physical and emotional challenges, such as walking a cable stretched thirty-five feet above the ground between two trees. We use similar events in our leadership development programs, as they do on many college campuses, to provide people with the opportunity to personally experience what it feels like to try something new. One lesson that emerges is that fear and apprehension are greater barriers to success than the actual difficulty or danger of the experiment itself. Randi puts it this way: "Self-imposed limitations and beliefs hold most people back. When individuals feel the surge of adrenaline and the thump of their hearts growing louder, they frequently interpret that feeling as fear. We encourage them to explore and to push on their perceived limits. By translating that feeling into excitement, they then discover the elation of victory over crippling doubts—and the ways they link these feelings back to their workplace are enormous."

Getting people to venture beyond the limitations that they normally place around themselves, to experience victory over doubt, is the key to their success. And this victory is key, for today's climate for colleges and universities demands a willingness to take risks and experiment with innovative ideas. Leaders foster risk taking, encouraging others to step out into the unknown rather than play it safe. They get to know the skills and motivations of their constituents. They set goals that are higher than current levels, but not so high that people feel only frustration. Leaders raise the bar gradually and offer coaching and training to build skills that help people get over each new level.

In our interviews and case studies we ask people to tell us about *personal-best leadership experiences.* Invariably, they elect to talk about times of change, underscoring the fact that leadership without change is entirely ceremonial. You can't manage yourself, the department, or institution to a better tomorrow without change.

SEIZE THE INITIATIVE

When we asked people to tell us who initiated the projects that they selected as their personal bests, we assumed that most would name themselves. Instead, more than half the cases were initiated by someone other than the leader—usually the person's immediate manager, department chair, director, or dean. Yet if leadership is about seizing the initiative, how can we call people leaders when they are assigned the jobs and tasks they undertake?

As we see it, the fact that over half the cases were not self-initiated is great news. It offers relief to the people who thought they had to initiate all the change and encouragement for the idea that responsibility for innovation and improvement is everyone's business. If the only times people reported doing their best were when they got to be the supervisor, department chair, some "head honcho," the majority of leadership experiences would evaporate—as would the majority of change on- and off-campus. The reality is that much of what people do is assigned; few of us get to start everything from scratch.

Seizing the initiative has absolutely nothing to do with position. It's about attitude and action. Innovation and excellence are the result of people at all levels making things happen. No surprise, then, to say that for innovation and continuous improvement, everyone needs to believe that they can make something happen. It's the responsibility of leaders to create the environment in which that belief can become a reality.

ENCOURAGE INITIATIVE IN OTHERS

Innovative leaders seize the initiative themselves and also encourage initiative in others. They want people to speak up, to offer suggestions for improvement, and to be straightforward about their constructive criticism. Yet when it comes to situations that involve high uncertainty, high risk, and high challenge, many people feel reluctant to act, afraid they might make matters worse.

Because of its high visibility, the annual "You Can Make A Difference" conference at Stanford University had been heavily micromanaged by various staff members—that is, until Jackie Schmidt-Posner became the adviser to the students running this conference. As she said, "I challenged our staff to walk our talk and support student development by empowering our students to carry out the project. We had to step back to let the students learn from their experience, even if they made some mistakes. This was risky because some of my colleagues felt the conference would not be of high quality if the students weren't closely monitored—and there was a chance they could've been right."

While Jackie admitted to being "a little nervous" at the start, she challenged the student leaders to excel by "constantly posing questions, asking them what their vision and goals were and how they could include and empower others to get there." She also encouraged and supported the students "to always learn from their experience." The conference was a huge success, involving and engaging large numbers of students and a significant diversity of students. A wider range of students assumed leadership roles than ever before. This program received a university-based award, while the two student coordinators received individual service awards from the university for their leadership.

Leaders, like Jackie, who speak out and challenge the status quo, have a belief in their ability to do something about the situation they face; they also believe in their ability to help others (Bandura, 1997; LePine and Dyne, 1998). People who are high in self-efficacy—who consider themselves capable of taking action in a specific situation—are more likely to act than those who are not. The most important way leaders create this can-do attitude is by providing opportunities for people to gain mastery on a task one step at a time. Training is crucial to building self-efficacy and to encouraging initiative. Isn't it interesting, perhaps ironic, that "training"—the *sin quo non* of higher education—is too infrequently applied to the development of faculty and staff capabilities?

Exemplary college and university leaders design and build in opportunities for learning by more than students. They fully appreciate that knowledge, like any institutional asset, deteriorates over time. They realize that people can't do what they don't know how to do, and short of firing everyone who doesn't come with all the skills intact—a virtual impossibility—you have to upgrade capabilities continuously. More and more higher education institutions are recognizing this by investing in administrative and management development programs for faculty and staff alike (Gillespie, 2002).

Leaders provide opportunities for people to exceed their previous levels of performance. They regularly set the bar higher. And the best leaders understand the importance of setting the bar at a level at which people feel they can succeed. Raise it too high, and people will fail; if they fail too often, they'll quit trying. Raise the bar a bit at a time, and eventually more and more people master the situation. This awareness of the human need for challenge and sensitivity to the human need to succeed are among the critical balancing skills of any leader.

MAKE CHALLENGE MEANINGFUL

We asked people to think of historical leaders who, if alive today, they would *willingly* follow. All of those nominated were people with strong beliefs about matters of principle. There's still another consistent thread: they were all individuals who served during times of turbulence, conflict, innovation, and change. They're people who triumphed against tremendous odds, who took initiative when there was inertia, who confronted tradition and the established order, who mobilized people and institutions in the face of strong resistance.

Leadership and challenge are inextricably linked, just as leadership and principles are inextricably linked. The implication is crystal clear. The leaders people admire are ones who have the *courage of their convictions.* What's even more important to constituents than having leaders with values is having leaders who stand up for those beliefs during times of intense challenge and radical change.

What gets *you* going in the morning, eager to embrace whatever might be in store? What motivates *you* to do your best, day in and day out? Why do people push their own limits to get extraordinary things done? And for that matter, why do people do many things for little or no tangible rewards? Extrinsic rewards—the traditional cliché of "what gets rewarded gets done"—certainly can't explain these actions in higher education. Institutions can't pay people to care about students, alumni, or even their colleagues; they can't pay people to care about their classes, programs, services, communities, families, or even the college's bottom line. People involved in higher education find satisfaction in efforts that don't pay a lot of money and have few special perks.

What gets people through the tough times, the times when they don't think they can even get up in the morning or take another step, give another lecture, make comments on another blue-book, write another article, generate another strategic report, refurbish another residence hall, attend another pep rally, baseball game, or concert, organize another reception, or hold another orientation, is a sense of meaning and purpose. The motivation to deal with the challenges and uncertainties of life and work comes from the inside and not from something that others hold out as some kind of carrot.

It's evident from our research, and from studies by many others, that if people are going to do their best, they must be *internally* motivated (Deci with Flaste, 1995). And this is nowhere more true than in higher education. The task or project in which they're engaged must be intrinsically engaging. When it comes to excellence, it's definitely *not* "what gets rewarded gets done"; it's "what *is* rewarding gets done." Leaders tap into people's hearts and minds. They get faculty and staff to understand, appreciate, and believe in the noble purposes of their specific organizational unit or department, within the context of the overall college's mission.

LOOK OUTWARD FOR FRESH IDEAS

When faced with new challenges people live with a high degree of ambiguity. Change and the accompanying uncertainty throw off customary equilibrium. Yet it's these fluctuations, disturbances, and imbalances that are the primary sources of creativity (Wheatley, 1992). Leaders must embrace innovation as they navigate their departments, programs, and institutions through what are becoming the permanent white waters surrounding higher education.

Leaders appreciate that improvements and innovations can come from just about anywhere. For example, some of the best new ideas for classes and program changes come from alumni. Technology applications often find their way onto college campuses after first being introduced in corporations. And changes in service-learning experiences at the secondary-school level have accelerated the scale and scope of university-based initiatives. Consequently, leaders must be actively looking and listening to what's going on around them for even the fuzziest sign or weakest signal that there's something new on the horizon.

Being innovative requires more listening and communication than does performing routine work. Guiding a change requires leaders to establish more relationships, connect with more sources of information, and to get out of their offices—even off their own campus—more frequently. This means staying in touch with trends in the academic and professional marketplaces, with the ideas and advice of people from a variety of backgrounds and disciplines, and with ongoing social, political, technological, economic, and artistic changes.

If leaders are going to detect opportunities for change—before those opportunities wither, become demands, or create huge problems—they must use their *outsight*. They must stay sensitive to the external realities. They must go out and talk to their constituents, be they local citizens, staff, employees, trustees, alumni, faculty, students, suppliers, vendors, managers, or just interested parties. They must listen—in person, on the phone, via e-mail, via web sites—and stay in touch.

INITIATE INCREMENTAL STEPS

If we're talking about challenging the process, why don't we start Big? Unfortunately, problems conceived of too broadly appear overwhelming. They often defeat our capacity to even think about what might be done, let alone begin taking action to solve them.

Leaders face a similar challenge: that mountain (or curriculum change, or shift in parking policy, or integration of marketing policies) looks much too high and difficult to climb; even taking the first steps can't be contemplated. Getting ourselves and others to exchange old mind-sets and habits for new ways of thinking and acting is daunting. Even with the best of intentions, people tend to revert to old and familiar patterns, especially in times of stress. Therefore, leaders need to get people to *want* to change the way they're currently headed on a one-step-at-a-time basis.

The most effective change processes are incremental; they break down big problems into small doable steps and get a person to say yes numerous times, not just once. Successful leaders help others to see how progress can be made by breaking the journey down into measurable goals and milestones. For example, on many college campuses faculty are being incrementally drawn outside of their academic silos (department and discipline-based units) by the creation of centers and programs created with a distinctive interdisciplinary and problem or application focus. Faculty who often resisted teaching in another department or school's program are agreeing to teach where their talents are most needed. With the need to provide more "faculty" advisers to first-year students (hence lowering the advisee-to-adviser ratio), campuses started turning to senior staff members to fulfill this mentoring role until students select academic majors. The use of staff in this capacity is selectively expanding, and creative ways to engage staff with the education of the whole person are emerging.

The academic community has always understood that major breakthroughs are likely to be the result of the work of scores of researchers, as countless contributions finally begin to add up to a solution. Advances in medicine or biophysics, for example, often involve many experiments focused on various pieces of the problem. Likewise, taking the sum total, all the "little" improvements in technology, regardless of the industry, have likely contributed to a greater increase in organizational productivity than all the great inventors and their inventions (Mintzberg, 1994).

Progress *today* is more likely to be the result of a focus on incremental improvements in tools and processes than of tectonic shifts of minds. Leaders keep the dream in mind; then they act and adapt on the move.

MAKE SMALL WINS WORK

This incremental change process can be called "small wins" as each success enables leaders to build peoples' commitment to a course of action. The alumni or development office does much the same thing when they ask graduating students and recent alumni for a small contribution. They know that it's easier to go back and request more in the future from those who've made an initial contribution than to return to someone who's never made a pledge. Leaders start with actions that are within their control, that are tangible, that are doable, and that can get the ball rolling.

The small wins process may not have initially been on Jeanne Rosenberger's mind as the dean of student life at Santa Clara University. But she put it to good use when she found herself as the link between the administration and a student group protesting SCU's acceptance of a $50,000 gift from a major government defense contractor. Jeanne needed to find a way to keep the protest from escalating, to assure everyone's safety, to safeguard the health of the students who were fasting as part of their protest, and to formulate a win-win.

Jeanne's aim was to create a calm, collaborative setting rather than a confrontational one. This, she managed step by step, gaining agreements and trust from both groups along the way. She made sure that a neutral location was used for meetings. She emphasized the importance of face-to-face communication and careful listening. She began each conversation with the students by asking about their health and well-being—not with an ultimatum. She gained the students' trust by advocating that the university call the local police or campus safety department only if needed, rather than having a constant police presence or threat of action.

As a result, the protest remained peaceful, the students fasted for four days—all with no health problems—and a dialogue began about the development of a gift policy. In addition, after the demonstration, Jeanne made use of the educational opportunities, involving students in reflecting on what they had learned—about the demonstration, about the university, about corporations, about themselves. Turning a protest into a learning opportunity—a teachable moment—required being open about the process and made it a win for everyone.

Small wins form the basis for a consistent pattern of accomplishment that attracts people who want to be allied with a successful venture. Small wins build people's confidence and reinforce their natural desire to feel successful. Since additional resources tend to flow to winners, this means that slightly larger steps or wins can be attempted next. A series of small wins therefore provides a foundation of stable building blocks. Each win preserves gains and makes it harder to return to preexisting conditions; each win also provides information that facilitates learning and adaptation.

Small wins also deter opposition for a simple reason: it's hard to argue against success. Thus small wins decrease resistance to subsequent proposals. In achieving a small win, leaders identify the place to get started. They make the project seem doable within existing skill and resource levels. This approach minimizes the cost of trying and reduces the risks of failing. Once a small win has been accomplished, natural forces are set in motion that favor stepping out toward another small win. This simple strategy of winning step by step succeeds while many massive overhauls and gigantic projects fail. It's not just that it's easier; it's also because it builds personal and group commitment.

LEARN FROM MISTAKES

The risks involved in a ropes course are like the risks leaders must take when involved in learning and in mastering change: making a mistake, or worse yet, failing. To be sure, failure can be costly. For the individual who leads a failed project, it can mean a stalled career or even a lost job. For the scholar, pursing a new avenue of research may result in failure to receive tenure and/or promotion. For the institute or center, it can lead to a loss of contracts and funding. For a dean or college president, it can mean a vote of "no confidence."

It is, however, absolutely essential to take risks. On the academic side, all scholarship, as in hypothesis testing, is an experiment in risk taking (such as explaining variance). On the staff side, few programs have ever gotten better by doing nothing. Over and over again, people in our study tell us how important mistakes and failure have been to their success. Without those experiences, they would have been unable to achieve their aspirations and breakthroughs. It may seem ironic, but many echo the thought that the overall quality of work improves when people have a chance to fail. Whatever the endeavor, the "learning curve" is not a straight line. Most innovations in fact might be called "failures in the middle" because we seldom learn without making mistakes first. Consider the times when you tried to learn a new game or a new sport. Maybe it was skiing, snowboarding, tennis, bridge, golf, hockey, inline skating, or the latest video game. Did you get it perfect the very first day? Not likely.

Nothing is ever done perfectly the first time—not in sports, not in games, and most certainly not in higher education. Our point isn't to promote failure for failure's sake, of course. We don't advocate for a moment that failure ought to be the *objective* of any endeavor. Instead, we advocate learning.

Leaders don't look for someone to blame when mistakes are made in the name of innovation. Instead, they ask, "What can be learned from the experience?" There's no simple test for determining the best tactic for learning. But it is clear that leaders approach each new and unfamiliar experience with a willingness to learn, an appreciation for the importance of learning, and a recognition that learning necessarily involves making some mistakes.

Nor is there a simple test for ascertaining the appropriate level of risk in a new venture. Costs and benefits, potential losses and potential gains must all be weighed. Knowing that one person's risk is another's routine activity, you must factor in the present skills of the team members and the demands of the task. But even if you could compute risk to the fifth decimal place, every innovation would still expose us to some peril. Perhaps the healthiest thing any of us can do is determine whether what we can learn is worth the cost. And it turns out that the ability to grow and learn under stressful, risk-abundant situations is highly dependent on how we view change.

PROMOTE PSYCHOLOGICAL HARDINESS

Uncertainty, risk, and mistakes are part of the price we pay for innovation, major improvements, and ultimately learning. But how do we learn to accept the inevitable failures and accompanying stress of innovation, and how do we help others to handle the stress of change? The personal bests shared with us, like the campus protest Jeanne faced or handing over the conference reins to the students as Jackie did, are clear examples of difficult, stressful projects—that generated enthusiasm and enjoyment. It isn't stress that makes us ill but how we respond to stressful events.

Intrigued by people who'd all experienced a high degree of stress but experienced varied degrees of illness, psychologists have hypothesized that individuals must have a distinctive attitude toward stress (Maddi, 1999). Studies of such "psychological hardiness," conducted across a wide variety of professions and occupations, have supported this viewpoint. There is a clear attitudinal difference between high-stress/high-illness people and high-stress/low-illness people. This latter group makes three very key assumptions about themselves in interaction with the world.

First, they feel a strong sense of *control,* believing that they can beneficially influence the direction and outcome of whatever is going on around them through their own efforts. Lapsing into powerlessness, feeling like a victim of circumstances, and passivity seem like a waste of time to them. Second, they are strong in *commitment,* believing that they can find something in whatever they are doing that seems interesting, important, or worthwhile. They are unlikely to engage in denial or feel disengaged, bored, and empty. Third, they feel strong in *challenge,* believing that personal improvement and fulfillment come through the continual process of learning from both negative and positive experiences. They feel that it is not only unrealistic but also stultifying to simply expect, or even wish for, easy comfort and security.

People with a hardy attitude take change, risk, turmoil, and the strains of life in stride. When they encounter a stressful event—whether positive or negative—they react predictably. They consider the event engaging, they feel that they can influence the outcome, and they see it as an opportunity for development.

How do you develop this hardy attitude and mind-set? It turns out that when there's a varied environment, many tasks involving moderate difficulty, and family support, then hardiness flourishes, regardless of socioeconomic background. But we shouldn't resign ourselves to a life of illness or unresolved stress if we didn't grow up in the right environment. Hardiness can be learned and cultivated at any time in life (Khoshaba and Maddi, 1999; Maddi, Kahn, and Maddi, 1998).

Leaders can help their constituents cope more effectively by creating a work climate that develops hardiness. For example, by choosing tasks that are challenging but within the person's skill level, they help build a sense of control. Offering more rewards than punishments to people fosters commitment. Encouraging people to see change as full of possibilities promotes an attitude of challenge.

People can't lead if they aren't psychologically hardy. No one will follow someone who avoids stressful events and won't take decisive action. However, even if leaders are personally very hardy, they can't enlist and retain others if they don't create an atmosphere that promotes psychological hardiness. People won't remain long with a cause that distresses them. To accept the challenge of change, they need to believe that they can overcome adversity. Leaders must create the conditions that make all of that possible.

The personal-best examples involved change and stressful events in the lives of leaders; they involved significant personal and organizational change. And nearly all of these cases were described in terms consistent with the conditions for psychological hardiness. No matter what the field, whether within or outside of higher education, leaders and their constituents experienced commitment rather than alienation, control rather than powerlessness, and challenge rather than threat.

It's instructive to know that people associate doing their best with feelings of meaningfulness, mastery, and stimulation, that people are biased in the direction of hardiness when thinking about their best. It's equally helpful to know that people don't produce excellence when feeling uninvolved, insignificant, and threatened. Furthermore, feelings of commitment, control, and challenge provide internal cues for recognizing when we're excelling and when we're only getting through the day.

CHALLENGING THE PROCESS

Whatever your position, the leadership attitude is one characterized by "wanting to make a difference." Of course, that's what every educator (faculty or staff) expects to accomplish within the purpose of higher education. Colleges and universities are not necessarily bastions of change; often quite the contrary. Still, within these hallowed halls, change is part of the institutional DNA. Our "customers" (students) will be changed by the institutional experience; otherwise, what's the point?

Challenging the process is not about change for the sake of change *per se* but consistent with higher education's purpose, change for the betterment. Leaders on college campuses are infused with making the status quo not simply different, but better. Making the current situation better demands change. To paraphrase Einstein, it would be foolish and foolhardy to expect things to be better simply by doing the same things over and over again.

Within and outside of higher education, when people talk about their personal-best leadership experiences, they talk about the challenge of change. When we look at leaders, we see that they're associated with transformations, whether small or large. Leaders don't have to change history, but they do have to make a change in "business as usual."

The quest for change is an adventure. It tests our skills and abilities. It brings forth talents that have been dormant. It's the training ground for leadership. Exemplary leaders, therefore, search for opportunities to make a difference—even when those opportunities are sometimes thrust upon them rather than chosen. They're always on the lookout for anything that lulls a group into a false sense of security; they constantly invite and create new initiatives. Leaders, by definition, are out in front of change, not behind it trying to catch up. The focus of a leader's attention should be less on the routine operations and much more on the untested and untried. Leaders should always be asking "What's new? What's next? What's better?" That's where the future is.

Leaders experiment and learn from their mistakes. A major leadership task involves identifying and removing self-imposed constraints and orga-

CHALLENGE THE PROCESS

- Seize the initiative
- Encourage initiative in others
- Make challenge meaningful
- Look outward for fresh ideas
- Initiate incremental steps
- Make small wins work
- Learn from mistakes
- Promote psychological hardiness

nizational conventions that block innovation and creativity. Yet innovation is always risky and leaders recognize failure as a necessary fact of the innovative life. Instead of punishing it, they encourage it; instead of trying to fix blame for mistakes, they learn from them; instead of adding rules, they encourage flexibility. Leaders are in the higher education business with a view of continuous improvement and lifelong learning.

Leaders have a hardy attitude about change. They venture outside the constraints of normal routine and experiment with creative and risky solutions. They create climates and communities so that faculty and staff alike can accept the challenge of becoming better. By having and fostering an attitude of psychological hardiness, leaders can turn the potential turmoil and stress of innovation and change into an adventure. By getting started, taking the first step, creating small wins, leaders set the stage, creating a climate and the conditions for turning their constituents into leaders themselves.

5

Enable Others to Act

CAROLYN BORNE IS PROGRAM DIRECTOR of the Women's Health Initiative (WHI) in the School of Medicine at the University of California, Los Angeles (UCLA). The WHI, part of a National Institutes of Health (NIH) study begun in 1991, is one of the largest and most ambitious longitudinal studies of postmenopausal women's health concerns ever undertaken, involving some forty-five centers across the United States and over 150,000 women. The study requires careful planning, analytical ability, and meticulous attention to detail, and, because of its sensitive and significant nature, it also requires a high degree of collaboration and trust.

But that climate didn't exist when Carolyn arrived. When she first joined as program director, during the recruitment phase of the study, the WHI group lacked collaboration, respect, and trust for each other. The emphasis seemed to be competition rather than cooperation and support. Hard as they were working, they were not at the expected national study goal for recruitment. Productivity and morale were low.

Carolyn took immediate steps to create a different kind of climate, a climate of trust and respect. She did a needs assessment, in which she interviewed each staff member. What she found was that the group was enthusiastic about the study but frustrated by the lack of systems, organization, and teamwork; in fact, she said, "Each member of the team was a talented professional, but each was ready to quit. They all liked their jobs but did not feel supported." Having identified the sources of frustration,

Carolyn's goal then became increasing group cohesion through improved communication. As Carolyn told us: "We started creating a team environment with a day-long retreat in which we began to identify our values, philosophy, and mission. We shared stories about families and loved ones and began to feel a sense of trust and respect for each other." Carolyn understood that to create a climate of collaboration and trust she needed to determine what the group needed, building the team around purpose and respect, and making each team member strong and efficacious.

In the thousands of cases we've studied, we've yet to encounter a single example of leadership that's occurred without the active involvement and support of many people. Likewise, we haven't found a single instance where creating competition between group members was the way to achieve the highest levels of performance. Quite the contrary, Carolyn and others like her spoke passionately about teamwork and cooperation as the interpersonal route to success, particularly when the conditions were extremely challenging and urgent. She understood her chief leadership challenge to be creating an environment in which the project staff could do their work successfully and collaboratively. She knew that for others to act at their best, they needed to trust each other.

CREATE A CLIMATE OF TRUST

Leaders put trust on the agenda; they don't leave it to chance. It's *the* central issue in human relationships within and outside organizations. Without trust you cannot lead. Individuals who are unable to trust others fail to become leaders precisely because they can't bear to be dependent on the words and work of others. So they either end up doing all the work themselves, or they supervise work so closely that they become overcontrolling. Their obvious lack of trust in others results in others' lack of trust in them.

What psychologists have found is that people who are trusting are more likely to be happy and psychologically adjusted than are those who view the world with suspicion and disrespect (Gurtman, 1992; Grace and Schill, 1986). People like those who are trusting and seek them out as friends. People listen to those they trust and accept their influence. Thus the most effective leadership situations are those in which each member of the team trusts the others.

Picture your faculty colleagues in a department meeting, your administrative colleagues in a program review meeting, or even a campuswide task force or governance committee. Now imagine that these people are involved in a role-playing exercise. They are given identical factual information about a difficult policy decision (such as program budget cuts) and then asked to solve a problem related to that information as a group. Half of the groups are briefed to expect trusting behavior ("You have learned from your past experiences that you can trust the other members and can openly express feelings and differences with them"); the other half, to expect untrusting behavior. Do you think you'll find differences in the ways the members of these two groups interact and problem solve with one another?

Actual studies like this one consistently show that the group members who'd been told that their role-playing peers and manager could be trusted reported their discussion and decisions to be significantly more positive than did the members of the low-trust group on *every* factor measured. Members of the high-trust groups were more open about their feelings, they experienced greater clarity about the group's basic problems and goals, they searched more for alternative courses of action, and they reported greater levels of mutual influence on outcomes, satisfaction with the meeting, motivation to implement decisions, and closeness as a management team as a result of the meeting.

In the group whose participants were told that their manager wasn't to be trusted, genuine attempts by the manager to be open and honest were ignored or distorted. Distrust was so strong that members viewed the manager's candor as a clever attempt to deceive them and generally reacted by sabotaging the manager's efforts even further. Managers who experienced rejection of their attempts to be trusting and open responded in kind. Not surprisingly, more than two-thirds of the participants in the low-trust group said that they would give serious consideration to looking for another position. People don't want to stay very long where there is no trust (Driscoll, 1978).

It's crucial to keep in mind that this was *a simulation;* the participants were role-playing. They behaved and responded as they did as a consequence of being told that they couldn't trust one another very much. Their actions showed that trust or distrust can come with a mere suggestion—and in mere minutes. To put it quite simply, trust is the most significant predictor of individuals' satisfaction with their organizations.

Trusting leaders allow people to be free to innovate and contribute; they nurture openness, involvement, personal satisfaction, and high levels of commitment to excellence. Knowing that trust is key, leaders make sure that they consider alternative viewpoints, and they make use of other people's expertise and abilities. Because they're more trusting of their groups, they're also more willing to let others exercise influence over group decisions. It's a reciprocal process. By demonstrating an openness to influence, leaders contribute to building the trust that enables their constituents to be more open to their influence. Trust begets trust.

FACILITATE POSITIVE INTERDEPENDENCE

At the beginning of the new millennium, millions tuned in to watch *Survivor,* the latest rage in "reality TV." With its competitive games, petty rivalries, backstabbing betrayals, tribal councils, and cliff-hanger endings, the show was a hit. During the peak weeks of the show, we found some of our clients using *Survivor* as a case study in how to be successful in any organizational setting.

To us, this was troubling. Riveting or not, *Survivor* and shows like it teach all the wrong lessons about how to survive in the "real world." In the real world, if people were to behave as these players on television did, they'd all be dead. As the acclaimed anthropologist Lionel Tiger put it, "The contest format distorted savagely what would have otherwise been a very different outcome involving ongoing cooperation. The behavior on the island . . . is a reflection of the nature of the prize, and what winning it demanded. The goal of human survival has always been to endure for another day, and in the group" (Tiger, 2000).

One of the most significant ingredients to cooperation and collaboration missing from *Survivor* was a sense of interdependence, a condition where everyone knows that they cannot succeed unless everyone else succeeds, or at least that they can't succeed unless they coordinate their efforts. If there's no sense that "we're all in this together," that the success of one depends on the success of the other, then it's virtually impossible to create the conditions for positive teamwork. To get extraordinary things done, people have to rely on each other. Leaders take an active role in creating a positive context and structure for cooperation and collaboration.

Susan Tomaro said that she always understood the importance of positive interactions but never more so than when she had the challenging assignment of planning the week-long orientation program for new students at Stanford University the year that this overlapped with the Jewish high holy days. Not only would there be conflicting events, but the two activities would be competing over the use of limited campus facilities. It was her first year in the position—and she immediately went to work building strong relationships with the Office of Religious Life and Hillel. Susan understood that there was little to be gained by either party trying to convince the other that their program was more important than the other's. What she did was to "provide information about the various challenges we all faced and seek everyone's help to change the way we would do things this time around. I asked people on all sides to think outside the box and recognize that the issues could only be resolved by getting many people involved and working together. Nobody was going to be successful without the support of everyone working together with one another." It's this ability to work together that leaders know is key.

DEVELOP COOPERATIVE GOALS AND ROLES

There were many leaders who were crucial to the successful development of the first doctoral program at the University of the Incarnate Word (San Antonio, Texas). Without their cooperative goals and roles, the change could never have happened. As Professor Charlie Slater explained to us, the president of the university started the ball rolling. Charlie and a small group of faculty then worked together to advocate for the program and to keep pushing the process along. Throughout the process, different individuals and groups enabled others through advocacy, reconciliation, or negotiation. For example, a veteran faculty member came forward at a key point. By emphasizing the group's shared beliefs, and couching them in moral terms, she was able to reconcile competing factions. Charlie explained that her efforts were "crucial to connecting the university's mission and values to the doctoral program." By helping faculty to acknowledge these shared beliefs, she enabled them to cooperate on syllabi and high-level goals for students, continuing their commitment to these tasks even amid other demands.

Whether it's a new doctoral program, campus housing, human resources, information technology, business services, or public safety, for a team of people to have a positive experience together, they must have shared goals that provide a specific reason for being together. No one can do it alone. A focus on a collective purpose binds people into cooperative efforts. Shared values and visions serve this function for the long term, and group goals provide this same common focus for the shorter term. Only through shared goals and recognized interdependence in one another's success can people create integrative solutions.

SUPPORT NORMS OF RECIPROCITY

In any effective long-term relationship, there must be a sense of mutuality. If one partner always gives and the other always takes, the one who gives will feel taken advantage of and the one who takes will feel superior. In that climate, cooperation is virtually impossible. To develop cooperative relationships, leaders must quickly establish norms of reciprocity among partners and within teams.

The power of reciprocity is dramatically demonstrated in the best-known study of the situation referred to as the "Prisoner's Dilemma." Two parties (individuals or groups) are confronted with a series of situations in which they must decide whether or not to cooperate. They don't know in advance what the other party will do. There are two basic strategies— cooperate or compete—and four possible outcomes based on the choices players make—win-lose, lose-win, lose-lose, and win-win.

The maximum individual payoff comes when one player selects a non-cooperative strategy and the other player chooses to cooperate in good faith. In this "I win but you lose" approach, one party gains at the other's expense. Although this might seem to be the most successful strategy—at least for the noncooperative player—it rarely proves to be successful in the long run, largely because the other player won't continue to cooperate in the face of the first player's noncooperative strategy. This typically leads to both parties deciding not to cooperate; attempting to maximize their respective individual payoffs, but in fact then both lose. When both parties choose to cooperate, both win, though the individual payoff for a cooperative move (win-win) is less than for a competitive one (win-lose) in the short run.

Researchers find, amazingly enough, that the most successful strategy is quite simple: cooperate on the first move and then do whatever the other player did on the previous move. How this strategy succeeds is by eliciting cooperation from others, not by defeating them (Poundstone, 1992). Simply put, people who reciprocate are more likely to be successful than those who try to maximize individual advantage.

The dilemmas that can be successfully solved by this strategy are by no means restricted to theoretical research. We all face similar dilemmas in our everyday lives:

- Should I try to maximize my own personal gain?
- What price might I pay for this action?
- Should I give up a little for the sake of others?
- Will others take advantage of me if I'm cooperative?

Reciprocity turns out to be the most successful approach for such daily decisions, because it demonstrates both a willingness to be cooperative and an unwillingness to be taken advantage of. As a long-term strategy, reciprocity minimizes the risk of escalation: if people know that you'll respond in kind, why would they start trouble? And if people know that you'll reciprocate, they know that the best way to deal with you is to cooperate and become recipients of your cooperation. Honor codes succeed on this principle, as do "good will" gestures between public safety and campus housing and negotiations between various faculty councils with their staff counterparts.

Reciprocity leads to predictability and stability in relationships, which can keep relationships and negotiations from breaking down (Cialdine, 2001). Part of the reason is that the knowledge that we share goals and will reciprocate in their attainment makes working together less stressful. Improved relationships and decreased stress: fine outcomes under any circumstances.

PROMOTE FACE-TO-FACE INTERACTIONS

Group goals, reciprocity, and rewarding joint efforts are all essential for collaboration to occur, but positive face-to-face interaction has the most powerful influence on whether those goals get achieved (Johnson and Johnson, 1989). This need for face-to-face communication increases with the complexity of the issues. For example, in working through many of the scheduling challenges around new student orientation Susan Tomaro had lots of one-on-one discussions with key players across the campus who could help think about the issues and create change. She "enlisted their help and worked collaboratively." In the end, Susan told us she became very good friends with a number of key partners, including the campus rabbi.

Leaders must provide frequent and lasting opportunities for team members to associate and intermingle across disciplines and between departments (or schools, colleges, programs, or divisions). Handy as virtual tools (such as e-mail and voice mail) are for staying in touch, they are no substitute for positive face-to-face interactions.

People who expect durable and frequent face-to-face interactions in the future are more likely to cooperate in the present. Knowing that we'll have to deal with someone in the future ensures that we won't easily forget about how we've treated, and been treated by, them. When durable interactions are frequent, the consequences of today's actions on tomorrow's dealings are that much more pronounced. In the end, durable relationships are more likely to produce collaboration than short-term ones.

PRODUCE SOCIAL CAPITAL

The new currency of the Internet Age isn't simply intellectual capital, it's *social capital*—the collective value of the people we know and what we'll do for each other. When social connections are strong and numerous there's more trust, reciprocity, information flow, collective action, and even happiness (Baker, 2000). Leaders, therefore, must make it a part of their personal agenda to get connected to the sources of information, resources, and influence they need to get extraordinary things done. They must also make sure that they connect their colleagues and constituents to each other and to those on the outside who are central to key networks. It'll make them more effective, more engaged in critical tasks, and more satisfied with their lives and work.

The most well-connected individuals are typically those who have been most involved in many campus activities. They haven't been typecast in one discipline, pedagogy, function, administrative body, or community. They've moved in and out of a range of assignments, committees, and experiences. They know people from a wide range of departments and programs, and have made connections across faculty, staff, and even student, alumni, and community domains. They've honed their interpersonal skills and knowledge so that they're credible to their constituents, and they've not dug themselves into a rut. Much as our college campuses are organized into discrete units, promoting specialization, when it comes to being a leader, you have to draw on your connections. If those connections are only in your specialty, it's likely that you'll be less influential than you can be if your connections cross a lot of boundaries. There's real long-term payoff in mining deep and wide when it comes to social connections.

In a world that is becoming more and more dependent on virtual connections, there's a temptation to believe that these connections automatically lead to greater trust. If we can reach across boundaries with the stroke of a key and the click of a mouse, we can more easily establish the foundation for better relationships. The hitch is, there really is no such thing as *virtual* trust (Cohen and Prusak, 2001).

Virtual trust, like virtual reality, is one step removed from the real thing. We are social animals; it's in our nature to want to interact face to face. If we didn't, we might as well abandon having faculty in the classroom altogether and simply let our wireless personal digital assistants do all the teaching. But bits and bytes make for a very weak social foundation. This may sound heretical in a world driving itself more and more to depend on electronic connections, but somehow we have to figure out how to combine and balance the benefits of technology with the social imperative of human contact. Data and information may be virtually shared, but we haven't yet worked out all the kinks to ensure understanding, sensitivity, knowledge, and action online or at a distance.

GENERATE POWER ALL AROUND

Exemplary leaders make other people feel strong. They enable others to take ownership of and responsibility for success by enhancing their competence and their confidence in their abilities, by listening to their ideas and acting upon them, by involving them in important decisions, and by acknowledging and giving credit for their contributions. Long before *empowerment* was written into the popular vocabulary, exemplary leaders understood how important it was that their constituents felt strong, capable, and efficacious.

Feeling powerful—literally feeling "able"—comes from a deep sense of being in control of life. People everywhere seem to share this: when we feel able to determine our own destiny, when we believe we're able to mobilize the resources and support necessary to complete a task, then we persist in our efforts to achieve. But when we feel we're controlled by others, when we believe that we lack support or resources, we show no commitment to excel (although we may comply). Thus any leadership practice that increases another's sense of self-confidence, self-determination, and personal effectiveness makes that person more powerful and greatly enhances the possibility of success (Bandura, 1997). Gallup surveys involving more than 1.5 million employees from over 87,000 work units clearly show that the extent to which people feel powerful and engaged in their work is directly linked to positive organizational outcomes, such as productivity and loyalty (Thackray, 2001; Buckingham and Coffman, 1999).

Creating a climate on campus where people are involved and important is at the heart of strengthening others. People must have the latitude to make decisions based on what they believe should be done. They must work in an environment that both builds their ability to perform a task or complete an assignment and promotes a sense of self-confidence in their judgment. People must experience a sense of personal accountability so that they can feel ownership for their achievements. Much of this in built into the job for members of the faculty, but not always. On the staff side, however, more attention to these enabling job dimensions is often required.

ENSURE SELF-LEADERSHIP

Leaders accept and act on the paradox of power: *we become most powerful when we give our own power away.* This is precisely what Mark DeLucchi told us in his personal-best leadership experience, which arose in connection with a Habitat for Humanity Collegiate Challenge at the University of Portland (Oregon). He explained how he gave students the power and the authority to carry out their jobs: "Although I tried to instill in them what I thought was important, I had them articulate what it was they wanted from this experience. I gave them the space and resources to achieve the goals as they defined them." Mark took this approach not simply with the group but with each individual. For example, when the student coordinator of the group came to him with a question, Mark's response was, "It's your show. What do you want to do?" Mark encouraged people to run with their ideas and to see what they came up with. If something went wrong, "I was right there to help them learn and then move on."

Traditional thinking promotes the archaic idea that power is a fixed sum: if I have more, then you have less. Naturally, people with this view hold tightly to the power that they perceive is theirs and are extremely reluctant to share it with anyone. This notion is wrongheaded and clearly inconsistent with all the evidence on high-performing organizations. As Mark found out, he didn't lose any influence with the group or on the project, because it "really was their show." Being a leader, Mark explained, "requires you to give up something. By giving some of the responsibility to others, they become invested and passionate about the project. Then my job becomes finding ways to help them see how it all comes together. But you've got to believe in the capabilities of your team to make this work."

Mark's viewpoint is supported by more than a quarter-century of research. The more people believe that they can influence and control the organization, the greater organizational effectiveness and member satisfaction will be. Shared power results in higher job fulfillment and performance throughout the organization (Borda, 1999; Williams and Wilson, 1997).

When leaders share power with others, they're demonstrating profound trust in and respect for others' abilities. When leaders help others to grow and develop, that help is reciprocated. People who feel capable of influencing their leaders are more strongly attached to those leaders and more committed to effectively carrying out their responsibilities. They *own* their jobs.

PROVIDE CHOICES

If leaders want higher levels of performance and greater initiative, they must be proactive in designing work that allows people discretion and choice. In other words, alternatives: being able to take nonroutine action, exercise independent judgment, and make decisions that affect how they do their work without having to check with someone else. Certainly the actions that Charlie Slater faced in developing that new doctoral program were far from routine. He made certain, accordingly, that any proposal he brought forth to various constituency groups (like the Faculty Senate) provided them with options from which to choose about how the program would be introduced and shaped. He did the same for the first group of students who were actually enrolled in the program prior to its formal approval. Kent Koth, in developing Willamette University's first alternate spring break, made certain that while everyone had the same "big picture" in mind, students had lots of decisions (choices) about how they would structure their daily activities, both on an individual as well as collective basis. In these ways, leaders, like Charlie and Kent, foster not only a sense of but actual ownership among those who will be responsible for the program or project's success and vitality.

Choice fuels our sense of power and control over our lives. Yet as necessary as choice is, it's insufficient. Without the knowledge, skills, information, and resources to do a job expertly, without feeling competent to skillfully execute the choices that it requires, people feel overwhelmed and disabled. Even if we have the resources, there may be times in which we aren't sure that we're allowed to utilize them, or that we'll be backed up if things don't go as well as expected. For those times, we need a well of competence and confidence.

BUILD COMPETENCE AND CONFIDENCE

Strengthening others requires up-front investments in initiatives that develop people's competencies and foster their confidence. Leaders know that if people are to feel strong, they must be honing and developing their skills and competencies. Leaders know they need to share information and resources with constituents. The confidence to do well is critical in the process of strengthening others. Just because individuals know *how* to do something doesn't necessarily mean that they *will* do it.

Enabling others to act is not just a practice or technique. It's a key step in a psychological process that affects individuals' intrinsic needs for self-determination. Each of us has an internal need to influence other people and life's events so as to experience some sense of order and stability in our lives. Feeling confident that we can adequately cope with events, situations, and people we confront puts us in a position to exercise leadership. Leaders take actions and create conditions that strengthen their constituents' self-esteem and internal sense of effectiveness.

Without sufficient self-confidence, people lack the conviction for taking on tough challenges. The lack of self-confidence manifests itself in feelings of helplessness, powerlessness, and crippling self-doubt.

Building self-confidence involves building people's inner strength to plunge ahead in uncharted terrain, to make tough choices, to face opposition and the like because they believe in their skills and in their decision-making abilities.

Empirical studies document how self-confidence can affect people's performance. In one study, participants were told that decision making was a skill developed through practice. The more one worked at it, the more capable one became. Another group of participants were told that decision making reflected their basic intellectual aptitude. The higher the underlying cognitive capacities, the better their decision-making ability. Both groups worked with a series of problems in a simulated organization. Participants who believed that decision making was an acquirable skill continued to set challenging goals for themselves, used good problem-solving strategies, and fostered organizational productivity. Their counterparts, who believed that decision-making ability was latent (that is, you either have it or you don't), lost confidence in themselves as they encountered difficulties. They lowered their aspirations for the organization, their problem solving deteriorated, and organizational productivity declined. Those participants who lost confidence in their own judgments tended to find fault with their people and were quite uncharitable about them, regarding them as unmotivatable and unworthy of supervisory effort. Given the option, they would have fired many of them (Wood and Bandura, 1989).

As these studies—and experience—underscore, having confidence and believing in your ability to handle the job, no matter how difficult, is essential in promoting and sustaining consistent efforts. Fostering self-confidence is not a warmed-over version of the power of positive thinking. Leaders communicate their belief that constituents can be successful; by doing so, leaders help people to extend themselves and to persevere.

FOSTER OWNERSHIP

A final key in making certain that people recognize their interdependency is through fostering ownership that builds accountability. The more people believe that everyone else is competent and taking responsibility for their own part of the job, the more trusting and the more cooperative they're going to be. It's also true that we'll be more confident in knowing that if we do our part, others will do theirs.

Unless people take personal responsibility and unless they are held accountable for their own actions, we're not very inclined to want to work with them nor much inclined to cooperate in general. Individual accountability is a critical element of every collaborative effort. Everyone has to do their part for a group to function effectively. Structuring the situation so that people have to work collaboratively can actually increase personal accountability. Why? Because we know that our peers are expecting us to be prepared and to do our jobs, and peer expectations are a powerful force in motivating us to do well. The feeling of not wanting to let the rest of the group down strengthens people's resolve to do their best.

Some people believe that teams and other cooperative endeavors minimize individual accountability. They believe that if we encourage people to work collectively, somehow they'll take less responsibility for their own actions than if we encourage them to compete or to do things on their own. It's true that some people become social loafers when in groups, slacking off while others do their jobs for them. But this doesn't last for long, because their team members quickly tire of carrying the extra load. The slacker either steps up to the responsibility, or the team wants that person out. Leaders know that part of their job is to set up conditions that enable each and every team member to feel a sense of ownership for the whole job.

ENABLING OTHERS TO ACT

"You can't do it alone" is the mantra of exemplary leaders—and for good reason. You simply can't get extraordinary things done by yourself. Fostering collaboration enables departments, programs, schools, and other alliances to function effectively. Collaboration can be sustained only when leaders promote a sense of mutual reliance—the feeling that we're all in this together. Mutual goals and roles contribute to mutual reliance, and the best incentive for others to help you in achieving your goals is knowing that you'll reciprocate, helping them in return. Help begets help just as trust begets trust. Focusing on what's to be gained fosters agreement in what might otherwise be divisive issues.

Leaders understand that there's no substitute for positive face-to-face interactions. Leaders help to create a trusting climate by the example they set. They also make sure that key constituents are able to make human contact; they work to make these interactions durable, and they connect people to the right sources of influence and information.

ENABLE OTHERS TO ACT

- Create a climate of trust
- Facilitate positive interdependence
- Develop cooperative goals and roles
- Support norms of reciprocity
- Promote face-to-face interactions
- Produce social capital
- Generate power all around
- Ensure self-leadership
- Provide choices
- Build competence and confidence
- Foster ownership

Strengthening others is essentially the process of turning constituents into leaders—making people capable of acting on their own initiative. Leaders strengthen others when they give their own power away to them, when they make it possible for constituents to exercise choice and discretion, when they develop in others the competence and confidence to act and to excel, and when they foster the accountability and responsibility that compels action. Exemplary leaders use their power in service of others because they know that capable and confident people perform better.

6

Encourage the Heart

THE CONFERENCE AND CATERING DEPARTMENT at the University of California, Los Angeles (UCLA) was preparing for its summer season—its busiest time—when it became aware that members of other departments on campus (such as physical plant, central receiving, and scheduling and facilities) were upset that they'd have to put out a great deal of effort to help Conference and Catering be successful but would receive very little in the way of rewards themselves. Mary Pat Hanker, director of Conference Services, knew that the department's success was dependent on the helpfulness of these other units and that she needed to gain their support, commitment, and involvement. She realized that the intervention had to be pleasant, playful, and humorous in order for people to want to participate (and to feel good about participating wholeheartedly rather than feeling threatened—and hence reluctant to participate).

So the Conference and Catering department staged a celebration—its employees held a barbeque for the people they were calling upon for help. Unlike most office parties, however, at this event the managers—the people responsible for generating the heavy summer business traffic—were the ones who cooked and served the food. Their symbolic reversal of roles did indeed foster a spirit of cooperation.

This summer barbeque celebration was separated from everyday work roles and work relationships. People across departments had the opportunity to interact with one another outside of the more formal and structured work context. The event gave people permission to interact with one another in a friendly and intimate manner, increasing their feelings of camaraderie and cooperation. It helped everyone appreciate the reasons behind the hectic summer season; it enhanced collaborative efforts and facilitated amiable interpersonal relationships throughout a stressful and highly productive period.

Mary Pat, like so many other leaders we talked with, came to understand the importance of recognizing people for who they are and celebrating what they contribute. In our personal-best case studies, people reported working very intensely and very long hours—and enjoying it. Yet to persist for months at such a pace, people need encouragement—and exemplary leaders are there to encourage people to do things that they have never done before.

Leaders give heart (the literal definition of courage) to others by recognizing individual contributions and celebrating victories together. Most people rate "having a caring boss" even higher than they value money or fringe benefits. In fact, how long employees stay at a company, and how productive they are there, is determined more by the relationship they have with their immediate supervisor than any other factor (Zipkin, 2000).

FOCUS ON CLEAR STANDARDS

Imagine Alice in Wonderland's frustrations when she played a croquet match where the flamingos were the mallets, the playing card soldiers were the wickets, and the hedgehogs were the balls. Everyone kept moving and the rules kept changing all the time. There was no way of knowing how to play the game to win (and it was rigged in favor of the Queen).

You needn't have gone down the rabbit hole to know how Alice felt: we've all been Alice at one time or another in our lives. We've all been at a place where we're not sure where we're supposed to be going, what the ground rules are that govern how we behave, or how we're doing along the way. And just when we think we get the hang of it, the organization comes along and changes everything. This is a recipe for maddening frustration and pitiful performance. Our hearts just aren't in it.

If leaders want their constituents to put their hearts into it, they must focus on clear standards. This is because the ideal experience—on or off the job—is to be in *flow*. Flow experiences are those times when we feel pure enjoyment and effortlessness in what we do (Csikzsentmihalyi, 1997). Experiencing flow requires clear standards (values and goals)—because they help us concentrate and avoid distractions. By having an intention to do something that is meaningful to us (for example, by setting a goal), we take action, action with a purpose.

Is it better that individuals set their own goals, or should leaders set the goals for others? In the best of all worlds, people would set their own. People feel best about themselves and what they do when they voluntarily do something; the worse feeling is when people are motivated because they have nothing else to do. This means that leaders have to make sure that whenever people engage in something, everyone knows why it's important and what end it's serving.

But standards and goals are not enough. People need to know if they're making progress toward the goal or simply marking time. People's motivation to increase their productivity on a task increases *only* when they have a challenging goal *and* receive feedback on their progress (Sawyer, Latham, Pritchard, and Bennett, 1999; Gostick and Elton, 2001). Goals without feedback, and feedback without goals, have little effect on motivation.

With clear goals and detailed feedback, people can become self-correcting and can more easily understand their place in the big picture. With feedback they can determine what help they need from others and who might be able to benefit from their assistance. Under these conditions they will be willing to put forth more productive effort.

In a study of the effects of feedback on self-confidence, graduate students were praised, criticized, or received no feedback on their performance in a simulation of creative problem solving. They had been told that their efforts would be compared with how well hundreds of others had done on the same task. Those who heard nothing about how well they did suffered as great a blow to their self-confidence as those who were criticized (McCarty, 1986). People hunger for feedback. They really do prefer to know how they are doing, and clearly no news has the same impact as bad news. This is one of the reasons why efforts to abolish grades in schools and colleges almost always fail.

EXPECT THE BEST

Successful leaders have high expectations, both of themselves and of their constituents. These expectations are powerful because they are the frames into which people fit reality. People are much more likely to see what they expect to see even when it differs from what may be actually occurring. There's ample research evidence that other people act in ways that are consistent with our expectations of them. If we expect others to fail, they probably will. If we expect them to succeed, they probably will (Eccles and others, 1998; Eden, 1992).

Our expectations also shape our own behavior, and, in turn, how we behave toward others. The high expectations that leaders have of others are based in large part on their expectations of themselves. This is one reason why leaders Model the Way. What gives their expectations for others credibility is their own record of achievement and dedication, and daily demonstrations of what and how things need to be accomplished.

Leaders treat people in a way that bolsters their self-confidence, making it possible for them to achieve more than they may have initially believed possible of themselves. Feeling appreciated by others increases a person's sense of self-worth, which in turn, precipitates success at school, work, and home. Research and everyday experience confirm that men and women with high self-esteem, of all ages and levels of education and socioeconomic backgrounds, "feel unique, competent, secure, empowered, and connected to the people around them" (Blitzer, Petersen, and Rogers, 1993, p. 59). If you have someone in your life who believes in you, and who constantly reinforces that belief through their interactions with you, you are strongly influenced by that support. If the potential exists within us, it will come out when a leader takes the time to bring us along.

BE POSITIVE

Positive expectations yield positive results. They create positive images in our minds and generate other positive possibilities. Positive futures for self and others are first constructed in our minds. "We see," say researchers, "what our imaginative horizon allows us to see" (Cooperrider, 1990,

p. 103). Seeing is believing, and the results can be life-affirming and life-enhancing.

Unless we can see ourselves as being successful, it is very difficult to produce the behavior that leads to success. Positive images make groups more effective, relieve symptoms of illness, and enhance achievement. As but one example, people were divided into different groups and instructed in effective bowling methods. Following these lessons, the bowlers practiced. Some of those who practiced were videotaped. One group of the videotaped bowlers saw only the positive things they did; the other group saw only the negative. Those who saw only their positive moves improved significantly more than any of the other bowlers and were more interested in continuing with the sport into the future (Cooperrider, 1990, p. 114).

Consider how this principle was put into practice by Kyle Von Raesfeld, a college freshman, who told us about his personal-best leadership experience: coaching a football team at an elementary school while he was only in high school himself.

My first year there I was an assistant coach. The head coach knew a lot about football. He probably would have been a good coach for older kids, but he did not stay very positive with the kids. He would always point out their mistakes and very seldom point out their successes.

It didn't take very long for the kids to start getting down on themselves. The coach seemed to be constantly shouting. Soon enough, attendance at practices started to drop. The kids had lost all of their desire to play the game, and they clearly were not having fun. We did not have a very successful season, not only in terms of win-loss record but also in accomplishing the primary goal, providing a good time for the kids.

The next year (through a series of circumstances), I was the head coach with a friend from high school as an assistant. I had the same kids from the year before, we played the same teams, ran the same plays—and this year we went undefeated. Even better than that, each kid improved greatly and had a great time playing football.

After we were a few weeks into the season I began to ponder why this team had basically done a 180-degree turnaround from the previous season. The first thing I noticed was that each kid had a big smile on his face as he came running out to practice. The kids were very enthusiastic about practice and always showed up. Why? I always made sure to keep a positive attitude. Where the previous coach would say, "Here's what you did wrong," I would say, "Here's what you guys did right," and then, "Here are two or three things you can improve upon."

I also required the kids to stay positive with each other. I had the players tell each other when they did something good and encourage each other when they make a mistake. Instead of hearing shouts of "Why didn't you catch it? That was an easy catch," a player would be greeted by "You'll get it next time." More often than not, he would catch the next pass!

Kyle had learned intuitively how high expectations lead to high performance. By focusing on positive images, he was able to noticeably change the way the kids felt about themselves and about others on the team. As he puts it, "If people feel like they've been defeated, whether it be from not receiving any praise, having a pessimistic leader, or comments from teammates, they will act and perform like they are defeated. But if you encourage and motivate them, more often than not, they will excel."

Clearly, before we can lead, we have to believe in others, and we have to believe in ourselves. Holding the belief that we and others can change and can develop new skills and abilities works magic on the constituents and on the leader that holds this perception.

PAY ATTENTION

Leaders are out and about all the time. They're attending meetings, visiting colleagues, touring around the campus, canvassing the student union, dropping in on the lab, making presentations at alumni association gatherings, holding roundtable discussions, speaking to community groups, or just dropping by colleagues' offices to say "Hello." Being mobile goes with the leader's territory.

This is not purposeless wandering. Leaders are out there for a reason. One of the reasons, we would maintain, is to show that you care. One way of showing you care is to *pay attention* to people, to what they are doing, and to how they are feeling. And if you are clear about the standards you're looking for and you believe and expect that people will perform like winners, then you're going to notice lots of examples of people doing things right and doing the right things.

Paying attention can't be from a distance—reading reports or hearing things secondhand. People we work with want to know who we are, how we feel, and whether we really care. They want to see us in living color. Since proximity is the single best predictor of whether two people will talk to one another, you have to get close to people if you're going to communicate. It means regularly walking the hallways, attending various campus events (social, athletic, theatrical, and so on), frequenting the relevant "water coolers" (that is, places to "hang out" informally with others, like the staff lounge, faculty club, student union, and such), and even hitting the road for frequent visits with counterparts on other campuses and institutions.

Another benefit from paying attention to the positive is that you're highly visible and you also make yourself known to others. While you're getting to know them, they're getting to know you. And who do you trust more, someone you know or someone you don't know? In general we're all much more likely to trust friends than strangers. Paying attention and actively appreciating others increases their trust in you. If others know you genuinely care about them, they're more likely to care about you.

BE A FRIEND

Managerial myth says we shouldn't get too close to our colleagues, we can't be friends with people at work. Well, set this myth aside. Over a five-year period, researchers observed groups of friends and groups of acquaintances (people who knew each other only vaguely) performing motor skill and decision-making tasks. The results were unequivocal. The groups composed of friends completed, on average, more than three times as many projects as the groups composed merely of acquaintances. In terms of decision-making assignments, groups of friends were over 20 percent more effective than groups of acquaintances were (Deal and Key, 1998, p. 5).

There is an important caveat, however. Friends have to be strongly committed to the group's goals. If not, then friends may not do better. This is precisely why it is so necessary for leaders to be clear about standards and to create a condition of shared vision and values. When it comes to performance, commitment to standards and good relations between people go together.

People are simply more willing to follow someone they like and trust. To become fully trusted we must trust. And that means being open: open to others, open *with* others. An open door is a physical demonstration of a willingness to let others in. So is an open heart. This means disclosing things about yourself. We don't mean tabloid-style disclosures. We mean talking about your hopes and dreams, your family and friends, your interests and your pursuits. We mean telling others the same things you'd like to know about them.

When we're open we make ourselves vulnerable—and this vulnerability makes us more human and more trusted. If neither person in a relationship takes the risk of trusting, at least a little, the relationship remains stalled at a low level of caution and suspicion. If leaders want the higher levels of performance that come with trust and collaboration, then they must demonstrate their trust *in* others before asking for trust *from* others.

This is something that Cathy Avila understood and put into practice as early as her first job after graduate school, when she was resident director of Castilian Hall at the University of California, Davis. She explained, "As a leader, I am an open book. I share very personal pieces of myself so that the people I lead have a thorough picture of my journey through life up until that point and will better understand how I work and why I work the way I do." Cathy soon discovered that when she demonstrated her trust in the residence staff by being the first to share personal information, challenges, goals, and fears, it made a big difference. For some staff, "it was the first time an adult (let alone their boss) had been honest and up-front with them." By opening her heart, she motivated each staff member to share their deeper selves with the group—and that they did throughout their time of working together.

Certainly, disclosing information about ourselves can be risky. We can't be certain that other people will like us, will appreciate our candor, will agree with our aspirations, will buy into our plans, or will interpret our words and actions in the way we intend. But, as Cathy did, by demonstrating the willingness to take such risks, leaders encourage others to take a similar risk—and thereby take the first steps necessary to find a common ground for building mutual trust.

PERSONALIZE RECOGNITION

A familiar complaint about recognition is that it's too often highly predictable, routine, and impersonal. A one-size-fits-all approach to recognition feels disingenuous, forced, and thoughtless. Over time it can even increase cynicism and actually damage credibility. That's why it's so important for leaders to pay attention to the likes and dislikes of each and every individual. To make recognition personally meaningful, leaders have to get to know their constituents. By personalizing recognition, they send the message that they took the time to notice the achievement, seek out the responsible individual, and personally deliver praise in a timely manner.

When Karyn Bechtel was transforming what she called a "bunch of fellowships into a fellowship program" at Stanford University, she made it a point to make personal connections between people's contributions as inputs to the selection process with the outcomes of their selections. Karyn wrote thank-you notes, personalizing each one. Beyond this, "During one afternoon staff break, I shared lists of selected fellows and showed how particular application materials and their specific recommendations were critical in the decision process." This personalized and public acknowledgment was a boost for everyone.

The extent to which recognition and rewards are applied to each individual in a personal (rather than an impersonal) manner also explains a lot about how leaders and their organizations get a motivational bang for their buck (or not) from recognizing people's contributions. After all, leaders get the best from others not by building fires under people but by building the fire within them.

What personalized recognition comes down to is *thoughtfulness*. It means taking those observations you've made about an individual and asking: "What would really make this special and unique for her? What could I do to make this a memorable experience so that he always remembers how important his contributions are?"

USE A CREATIVE MIX OF REWARDS

Don't make the mistake of assuming that individuals respond only to money. Although salary increases or bonuses are certainly appreciated, individual needs for and appreciation of rewards extend much further. Verbal recognition of performance in front of one's peers and visible awards, such as certificates, plaques, and other tangible gifts, are powerful indeed and almost unlimited.

Spontaneous and unexpected rewards are often more meaningful than the expected formal rewards. In addition, relying upon an organization's formal reward system typically requires considerably greater effort than making use of *intrinsic* rewards—rewards that are built into the work itself, including such factors as a sense of accomplishment, a chance to be creative, and the challenge of the work. These rewards are far more important than salary and fringe benefits in improving job satisfaction, commitment, retention, and performance (Bond, Galinsky, and Swanberg, 1998). Often it's the simple, personal gestures that are the most powerful rewards. It's true that money may get people to do the job, but it doesn't necessarily get them to do a *good* job.

Praise and coaching are significant forms of recognition. Not enough people make enough use of one powerful but inexpensive two-word reward—"thank you." Personal congratulations rank at the top of the most powerful nonfinancial motivators identified by employees (Nelson, 1996).

There are few if any more basic needs than to be noticed, recognized, and appreciated for our efforts. And that's as true for academics, engineers, artists, counselors, residence advisers, budget analysts, and athletic coaches as it is for the physical plant staff and those in the president's office. There's little wonder, then, that the greatest volume of thanks is reported in the most highly innovative organizations.

CREATE A SPIRIT OF COMMUNITY

All over the world, in every country, in every culture, people stop working on certain days during the year and take the time to celebrate. Impromptu ceremonies are convened in the conference room to rejoice in the acceptance of a colleague's manuscript for publication or the award of a new contract for the department. Banquets are attended to show our respect for individuals and groups who've accomplished the extraordinary. Colleagues get together with one another at the end of a grueling work session and give each other high-fives for a job well done. Even in tragic times people come together in remembrance and song to honor those before us and to reaffirm our common humanity.

Why do we take time away from working to come together, tell stories, and raise our spirits? Sure, we all need a break from the pace and intensity of our jobs, but celebrations are not trivial excuses to goof off. Celebrations are among the most significant ways we have to proclaim our respect and gratitude, to renew our sense of community, and to remind ourselves of the values and history that bind us together. Celebrations serve as important a purpose in the long-term health of our institutions as does the daily performance of tasks.

What leaders know from practice is confirmed in our research. Performance improves when leaders bring people together to rejoice in their achievements and to reinforce their shared principles. By bringing people together, sharing the lessons from success, and getting personally involved, leaders reinforce in others the courage required to get extraordinary things done in organizations.

Individual recognition increases the recipient's sense of worth, and it improves performance. Public celebrations have this effect and more. Every gathering of a group is a chance to renew commitment. Leaders seldom let pass any opportunity to make sure that everyone knows why they're all there and how they're going to act in service of that purpose.

Whether it's in honor of an individual, group, or organizational achievement, celebrations offer leaders the perfect opportunity to explicitly communicate and reinforce the actions and behaviors that are important in realizing shared values and shared goals.

Celebrations are much more than parties; they're ceremonies and rituals that create meaning. It's vitally important to be clear about the statements you're making and the behaviors you're reinforcing at these occasions. You should be fully aware that people are going to leave the event remembering and repeating what you say and what they see. You should always be personally prepared with the key messages you want to send. Constantly ask yourself, "What values do we hold dear, what visions to we aspire to realize, and what behaviors do we want to reinforce?" Be prepared for every public opportunity to reinforce the culture and the meaning you want to create.

PROVIDE SOCIAL SUPPORT

Ceremonies and celebrations are opportunities to build healthier groups, to enable members of the organization to know and care about each other. And supportive relationships at work—relationships characterized by a genuine belief in and advocacy for the interests of others—are critically important to maintaining personal and organizational vitality.

One of the significant lessons learned from an extensive ten-year study of service quality is that social support networks are essential for sustaining the motivation to serve. Service-performance shortfalls are highly correlated with the absence of social support and teamwork: "Coworkers who support each other and achieve together can be an antidote to service burnout. . . . Working with others should be rejuvenating, inspirational, and fun" (Berry, Parasuraman, and Zeithaml, 1994).

Strong human connections produce spectacular results. Our studies confirm that extraordinary accomplishments are achieved when leader and constituents alike get personally involved with the task and with other people. When people feel a strong sense of affiliation and attachment to their colleagues they're much more likely to have a higher sense of personal well-being, to feel more committed to the organization, and to perform at higher levels. When they feel distant and detached they're unlikely to get anything done at all.

Leaders understand that what makes us most miserable is being alone. Knowing that we aren't alone in our efforts and that we can count on others if necessary helps build the courage to continue in times of turmoil and stress. The case for social support is also bolstered by the fact that information exchange is more likely to be facilitated, whether in formal or informal interactions, when people like one another. Even in the age of the Internet, people are just more likely to share things when they're in a gathering with other people than when they're sitting alone at their work stations. When celebrations cut across functional and hierarchical boundaries (as Mary Pat Hanker's summer barbeque did), people get a chance to exchange ideas with and be stimulated by people outside their own specialties

SET THE EXAMPLE

Wherever you find a strong culture built around strong values you'll also find endless examples of leaders who personally live the values. Whether it's the resident adviser who chooses the less desirable suite because it's closer to the main hub of the residence hall, the faculty member who works all weekend to get papers returned to students in a timely manner, or the academic administrator who continues to teach classes to stay in touch with the students, leaders make their values tangible by putting them into action. It's the same with encouraging the heart, whether through individual recognition or group celebration; the leader has to set the example.

The only way to truly show people you care and that you appreciate their efforts is to be out there with them. You've got to walk the corridors, stroll around the residence halls, eat in the cafeteria, wander through the library, listen to complaints, and tell stories about successes. Such visibility makes you vulnerable and at the same time makes you more real and more genuine. Authenticity goes up when you get personally involved. By directly and visibly showing others that you're there to cheer them along, you're sending a positive signal. You're more likely to see others do it if you do it. It's that simple.

Because leadership is a relationship, people are much more likely to enlist in initiatives led by those with whom they feel a personal affiliation. It's precisely the human connection between leaders and constituents that ensures more commitment and more support. Saying thank you—and genuinely meaning it—is a very concrete way of showing respect and enhancing personal credibility.

As we approach the end of our Five Practices of Exemplary Leadership story we've come full circle. We started our discussion of personal-best leadership with Model the Way—and here we are again. If you want others to believe in something and behave according to those beliefs, you have to set the example. You have to practice what you preach. If you want people to stay true to shared values, you have to stay true to them as well. If you want to build and maintain a culture of excellence and distinction, then you have to recognize, reward, reinforce and celebrate exceptional efforts and successes. You have to get personally involved in celebrating the actions that contribute to and sustain the culture. And if you want people to have the courage to continue the quest in the face of great adversity, you have to encourage them yourself.

ENCOURAGING THE HEART

Leaders have high expectations of themselves and expect the best of their constituents. Their standards are clear and these help people focus on what needs to be done. Leaders provide clear directions, feedback, and encouragement. By paying attention, offering encouragement, personalizing appreciation, and maintaining a positive outlook leaders stimulate, rekindle, and focus people's energies and drive.

Leaders make people winners, and winning people like to up the ante, raise the standards, and explore uncharted territory. Leaders recognize individual contributions to vision and values. And leaders express their appreciation far beyond the limits of the organization's formal performance appraisal system. Leaders enjoy being spontaneous and creative in saying thank you, by sending notes, handing out personalized prizes, listening without interrupting, and by a myriad number of other forms of recognition.

ENCOURAGE THE HEART

- Focus on clear standards
- Expect the best
- Be positive
- Pay attention
- Be a friend
- Personalize recognition
- Use a creative mix of rewards
- Create a spirit of community
- Provide social support
- Set the example

Celebrating values and victories together reinforces the fact that extraordinary performance is the result of many people's efforts. By celebrating people's accomplishments visibly and in group settings, leaders create and sustain team spirit; by basing celebrations on the accomplishment of key values and milestones, they sustain people's focus.

Public ceremonies provide opportunities to reiterate key values and to make heroes and heroines of individuals with whom everyone can identify. Telling stories about individuals who have made exceptional efforts and achieved phenomenal successes provides role models for others to emulate. Social interaction increases people's commitments to the standards of the group and has a profound effect on people's well-being.

Leaders who set the example by getting personally involved in celebration and recognition let everyone know that encouraging the heart is something everyone should do. Making personal connections with people in a culture of celebration also builds and sustains credibility.

7

Leadership Is Everyone's Business

BEYOND THE PRACTICES, beyond the action steps, there's another fundamental truth about leadership: *leadership is everyone's business.* This is as true in institutions of higher learning as it is in manufacturing, high technology, health care, government, military services, and not-for-profit agencies. In any organization, the best leaders understand this. They feel strongly about an issue, a cause, a program and find ways to share that feeling and involve people in making the extraordinary happen.

When John Seybolt was the dean of the School of Business at the University of Utah, he came to have a clear view of the school's future. He knew that, given the extremely high competition for outstanding faculty, the school needed major new sources of external funding. As he told us, "My fondest dream at the time was that we would receive a significant endowment for the school, giving it the freedom and flexibility to fund people and projects that could really make a difference. I also dreamed that because of these gifts, people would 'stand up and take notice' of the school and its potential." The school had long been referred to as "a hidden treasure." John countered that statement by saying "a hidden treasure is just that . . . HIDDEN . . . and that's not what we want to be."

John talked a lot about what private funding sources could mean to the school. He spread the feeling that "this is an exciting time" and "what I can do here will make a difference." He challenged the status quo by asking people to do some things they had never done before, whether it meant having faculty members speak with local community and business leaders about the importance of their research or asking community leaders to work with the school in new ways. Similarly he involved faculty, students, and alumni in imagining the future possibilities for the school that an endowment could create.

Ultimately the school received an endowment of $15 million from a single individual, earmarked to "build and sustain the intellectual infrastructure" of the school, renamed as the University of Utah's David Eccles School of Business. The endowment was, at the time, among the ten largest single gifts ever to a business school in the U.S., and the largest single gift in the history of the state.

When asked if he and his group received any special recognition for their efforts, John's answer was telling: "We received the greatest reward possible: a financial security blanket designed to help ensure that the school would be able to continue to attract and retain prominent faculty members, outstanding students, and provide seed funding for innovative programs that would enable it to thrive." John described the "reward" in terms of benefiting the school at large, and not for himself, or even any one group of constituents. How's that for putting the "we" first!

Boiled down, it sounds easy. But it wasn't. The school had never focused a lot of attention on significant fundraising; it was, after all, part of a state (public) university. Yet John was driven in his quest—and he was not alone. He involved and mobilized others on campus and off— he modeled, inspired, challenged, enabled, and encouraged—all along the way.

Like John, many of the people we studied became leaders as they simply believed they could make something better than it was or had been. They saw an opportunity where others didn't; they seized upon a possibility where others had been discouraged by the probabilities. They mobilized others in behalf of a cause and shared the necessary resources so that others could become leaders in their own right. Not every leader initiated the personal-best leadership projects that they wrote and talked about, yet they rose to the occasion. Some got angry and caught fire. Some accepted an assignment and then found something within themselves that they hadn't known they had. None of us knows our true strength until challenged to bring it forth. We're all like tea bags, not knowing how strong we can be until we're in hot water!

LEADERSHIP IS LEARNED

There persists a pernicious myth that leadership is reserved for only a very few of us. That myth is perpetuated daily every time someone asks, "Are leaders born or made?" Whenever people ask us this question—which is almost every time we give a speech or conduct a class or workshop—our answer, always offered with a smile, is this: "Yes, of course, *all* leaders are born. So are all college presidents, deans, coaches, teachers, scholars, registrars, directors, actors, accountants, artists, parents, you name it." We're all born with various sets of skills and abilities. What we do with what we have before we die is up to us.

There's another leadership myth that stands in the way of personal and organizational success. It's the myth that leadership is associated with position. It's an assumption that leadership starts with a capital L and that when you're on top you're automatically a leader. This view is part of a larger hero myth that inhibits people from seizing the initiative and keeps them waiting for someone to ride in and save the day.

Well, it's pure myth that only a lucky few can ever understand the intricacies of leadership. Leadership is not a place, it's not a gene, and it's not a secret code. The truth is that leadership is an observable set of skills and abilities that are useful whether one is in the chancellor's office, the bookstore, library, classroom, dining hall, residential learning community, human resources, public safety, information technology, or student services. Any skill, like leadership, can be strengthened, honed, and enhanced, given the motivation and desire, through practice and feedback, and with good role models and coaching. So, all leaders are born *and* all leaders are made.

It's very curious and revealing that no one has ever asked us, "Can *management* be taught? Are *managers* born or made?" Why is management viewed as a set of skills and abilities, while leadership is typically seen as a set of innate personality characteristics? It's simple. People *assume* management can be taught. Because they do, hundreds of business schools have been established, and each year thousands of management courses are taught. By assuming that people can learn the attitudes, skills, and knowledge associated with good management practices, schools and companies have raised the caliber of managers. They've also contributed to the idea that good management skills are attainable.

The same can be said for leadership. It's not the absence of leadership potential that inhibits the development of more leaders; it's the persistence of the myth that leadership can't be taught and leadership can't be learned. This haunting myth is a far more powerful deterrent to leadership development than is the nature of the person or the basics of the leadership process. And clearly this myth is antithetical to the essence of any educational philosophy.

It's our collective task to liberate the leader within each and every one of us. Rather than view leadership as an innate set of character traits— a self-fulfilling prophecy that dooms each campus and society at large to having only a few good leaders—it's far healthier and more productive to assume that it's possible for *everyone* to learn to lead. By assuming that leadership is learnable, we can discover how many good leaders there really are. Somewhere, sometime, the leader within each of us may get the call to step forward—for the department, the school, the program, the college, as well as for our families, congregations, neighborhoods, and communities. By believing in yourself and your capacity to learn to lead, you make sure you'll be prepared when that call comes.

Certainly, we shouldn't mislead people into believing that they can attain unrealistic goals. However, neither should we assume that only a few can ever attain excellence in leadership (or in any other human endeavor). We do know that those who are most successful at bringing out the best in others are those who set achievable "stretch" goals and believe that they have the ability to develop the talents of others. We do know that effective leaders are constantly learning. They see *all* experiences as *learning* experiences, not just those sessions in a formal classroom or workshop. They're constantly looking for ways to improve themselves and their organizations. By reading this book and engaging in other personal development activities, you're demonstrating a predisposition to lead. Even if some people think that they're not able to learn to lead, you must believe that you can. That's where it all starts—with your own belief in yourself.

CONTRASTS AND CONTRADICTIONS

In our research we identified the Five Practices of Exemplary Leadership. We learned that in performing at their personal bests, leaders Model the Way, Inspire a Shared Vision, Challenge the Process, Enable Others to Act, and Encourage the Heart. And we, along with other scholars, have found that leaders who more frequently engage in the Five Practices are significantly more likely to achieve extraordinary results than leaders who make use of these practices less often. Exemplary leadership and credible leaders make a difference in the world.

But there's catch. Any leadership practice *can* become destructive. Virtues can become vices. There's a point at which each of the Five Practices, taken to extremes, can lead you astray. Finding your voice and setting an example are essential to credibility and accomplishment—but an obsession with being seen as a role model can lead to being too focused on your own values and your way of doing things. It can cause you to discount others' views and be closed to feedback. It can push you into isolation for fear of losing privacy or being "found out"; it can also cause you to be more concerned with style than substance.

Being forward-looking and communicating a clear and common vision of the future set leaders apart from other credible people. Yet a singular focus on one vision of the future can blind you to other possibilities as well as to the realities of the present. It can cause you to miss the exciting possibilities that are just out of your sight or make you hang on just a little too long to an old, tired, and out-of-date technology. Exploiting your powers of inspiration can cause others to surrender their will. Your own energy, enthusiasm, and charm may be so magnetic that others don't think for themselves.

Challenging the process is essential to promoting innovation and progressive change. Seizing the initiative and taking risks are necessary for learning and continuous improvement. But take this to extremes and you can create needless turmoil, confusion, and paranoia. Routines are important, and if you seldom give people the opportunity to gain confidence and competence they'll lose their motivation to try new things. Change for change's sake can be just as demoralizing as complacency.

Collaboration and teamwork are essential to getting extraordinary things done in today's turbulent world. Innovation depends on high degrees of trust. And people must be given the power to be in control of their own lives if they are to accomplish great things. But an over-reliance on collaboration and trust may reflect an avoidance of critical decisions or cause errors in judgment. It may be a way of *not* taking charge when the situation requires. Delegating power and responsibility can become a way of dumping too much on others when they're not fully prepared to handle it.

People do perform at higher levels when they're encouraged. Personal recognition and group celebration create the spirit and momentum that can carry a group forward even during the toughest of challenges. At the same time a constant focus on who should be recognized and when we should celebrate can turn us into gregarious minstrels. We can lose sight of the mission because we're having so much fun. Don't become consumed by all the perks and pleasures and forget the purpose of it all.

Far more insidious than all of these potential problems, however, is the treachery of hubris. It's fun to be a leader, gratifying to have influence, and exhilarating to have scores of people cheering your every word. In many all-too-subtle ways, it's easy to be seduced by power and importance. All evil leaders have been infected with the disease of hubris, becoming bloated with an exaggerated sense of self and pursuing their own sinister ends. How then to avoid it?

Humility. You can avoid excessive pride only if you recognize that you don't know everything, that there are other smart, talented, experienced, and dedicated people. Knowing that you're only human helps, as does recognizing that nothing great was ever accomplished alone—that we all need the help of others. In the context of education, it's only fitting to note that leaders are great learners. Listen to what your colleagues have to say. Find the honesty to admit your mistakes and the grace to step back, correcting, and forgiving yourself. Hold onto humility: it's the only way we know to resolve the conflicts and contradictions of leadership.

In fact, research on companies that transition from mediocrity (or worse) to long-term superiority reveals a remarkable pattern of humility among the chief executives of "good-to-great" companies: "In contrast to the *I*-centric style of the comparison leaders, we were struck by how the good-to-great leaders *didn't* talk about themselves . . . they'd talk about the company and the contributions of other executives as long as we'd like but would deflect discussion about their own contributions" (Collins, 2002, p. 27). Similarly, their compelling modesty is perhaps why many of the best leaders within higher education are not the ones to grab the headlines in the *Chronicle of Higher Education,* the local or national press, or gain rock-star status in the popular leader-as-hero culture. Instead, these leaders focus their attention and will on their institutions and on others.

This is consistent with our own findings. The leaders in higher education we met, like John Seybolt, cared more about the institution than they did about their own successes. As we've discussed, exemplary leaders know that "you can't do it alone" and they act accordingly. They lack the pride and pretense displayed by many people who succeed in the short term but leave behind a weak organization that fails to remain strong after their departure. Instead, with self-effacing humor and generous and sincere credit to others they get higher and higher levels of achievement; they get extraordinary things done.

There's another way to avoid the temptations of power that lead to becoming overbearing and presumptuous. Refuse to become one-dimensional, focused narrowly on your work; do not allow work to consume you. Get involved in the world that surrounds you. The very best leaders have numerous pursuits and interests—arts, literature, science, technology, entertainment, sports, politics, law, religion, friends, and family.

There's one other important lesson here. Nothing in our research even hints that leaders should be perfect. Leaders aren't saints. They're human beings, full of flaws and failings like the rest of us. They make mistakes. Perhaps the very best advice we can give all aspiring leaders is to adopt the attitude of a novice—to always remain open and full of wonder. The best leaders, as we've said, are the best learners.

KEEP HOPE ALIVE

People look for leaders who demonstrate an enthusiastic and genuine belief in the capacity of others, who strengthen people's will, who supply the means to achieve, and who express optimism for the future. People want leaders who remain passionate despite obstacles and setbacks. Leaders throughout our colleges and universities with a positive, confident, can-do approach to life and the business of higher education are desperately needed.

Being at our personal best as leaders was, and is, never an easy or simple experience. Everyone we talked with acknowledged the hard work, the disappointments, the setbacks and mistakes, the misgivings and the sacrifices that were required, whether the task was curriculum review (such as a new set of requirements for a departmental major or a new first-year core across the college), revising the faculty handbook, establishing a new service-learning program, moving from the concept of "dormitories" to residential learning communities, building a new twenty-first century library (for example, should it have books in it?), holistically integrating student affairs programs with the academic affairs programs, requiring a common platform across the campus for information services and technology, bringing alumni and development programs under one common roof, or determining a comprehensive marketing strategy for the campus. Leaders in every one of these situations needed to keep hope alive, even in the most difficult of times. They had to strengthen their constituents' belief that today's struggle would produce a more promising tomorrow. Leaders demonstrate their faith and confidence by holding themselves accountable, by not asking anyone else to do something they wouldn't be willing to do themselves, and by accepting responsibility for the quality of the lives of their constituents and colleagues, programs, departments, and even institutions. Even when everything goes wrong or when they suffer resounding defeats, leaders display constancy and unwavering commitment to the cause.

"I knew in my heart what we were trying to do, and why we were trying to do it, and what I was prepared to do myself to make it happen" is a phrase repeated over and over again by those who provide leadership in higher education. Jeanne Rosenberger didn't give up on her belief that the students would live up to their responsibility. Alan Glassman never stopped believing that his faculty colleagues across the campus could work collectively in the strategic planning process with the central administration to rebuild and revitalize the university. Dennis Dow continues to believe—and champions that belief—that the counseling center contributes not simply to students' well-being but to the vitality of the campus. Kent Koth pioneered an alternative spring break program and didn't ask of his students anything he wasn't already doing or willing to do in service to others. Les Cochran moved his family into the deteriorating and gang-infested neighborhood that had come to surround the college campus; this brave action gave resounding testimony to his words "together we can make a difference."

Without hope there can be no courage—and college and university settings are not the place for the timid. This is the time and place for optimism, imagination, and enthusiasm. Leaders must summon their will if they are to mobilize the personal and organizational resources to triumph against the odds. Hope is essential to achieving the highest levels of performance. Hope enables people to transcend the difficulties of today and envision the potentialities of tomorrow. Hope enables people to bounce back even after being stressed, stretched, and depressed. Hope enables people to find the will and the way to aspire to greatness. And yet, hope is not all.

THE SECRET TO SUCCESS IN LIFE

Early in our study of leadership bests we were fortunate to cross paths with U.S. Army Major General John H. Stanford. We knew that he had survived military tours in Vietnam and was highly decorated and that the loyalty of his troops was unflagging. He would go on to head up the Military Traffic Management Command for the U.S. Army. Following his military career, he became the chief county administrator for Fulton County (which includes Atlanta, Georgia) as it geared up to host the 1996 Summer Olympics. He was subsequently recruited to the position of superintendent for the Seattle, Washington school system, where he sparked a revolution in public education.

John was a renaissance individual, who had served at the local, national, and international levels, whose distinguished career transcended and bridged the armed services, public administration, and educational systems. His answer to one of our interview questions significantly influenced our understanding of leadership at the deepest level. He gave voice to how we saw him live his life.

What we asked John was how he would go about developing leaders, whether at a college or university, in the military, in government, in the nonprofit sector, or in private business. Here's what he told us:

> *When anyone asks me that question, I tell them I have the secret to success in life. The secret to success is to stay in love. Staying in love gives you the fire to ignite other people, to see inside other people, to have a greater desire to get things done than other people. A person who is not in love doesn't really feel the kind of excitement that helps them to get ahead and to lead others and to achieve. I don't know any other fire, any other thing in life that is more exhilarating and is more positive a feeling than love is.*

"Staying in love" isn't the answer we expected to get—at least not when we *began* our study of leadership. But after numerous interviews and case analyses, we were struck by how many leaders used the word *love* freely when talking about their own motivations to lead, in explaining why they endured the hardships, made the personal sacrifices, and accomplished what they did.

Of all the things that sustain a leader over time, love is the most lasting. It's hard to imagine leaders on any college campus getting up day after day, and putting in the long hours and hard work it takes to get extraordinary things done, without having their hearts in it. This may just be the best-kept secret of successful leaders: If you love what you're doing, you will never have to work. Stay in love with leading, stay in love with the people who do the work, with the students, faculty, staff, and alumni that are transformed because of their time at your institution, with the scholarship, ideas, programs, and applications that emerge through and because of what you and so many others contribute.

Leadership is *not* an affair of the head. Leadership is, after all, an affair of the heart.

REFERENCES

Astin, A. W., and Astin, H. S. *Leadership Reconsidered: Engaging Higher Education in Social Change.* Battle Creek, Mich.: W. K. Kellogg Foundation, 2000.

Baker, W. *Achieving Success Through Social Capital: Tapping the Hidden Resources in Your Personal and Business Networks.* San Francisco: Jossey-Bass, 2000.

Bandura, A. *Self-Efficacy: The Exercise of Control.* New York: W. H. Freeman, 1997.

Bass, B. M. *Leadership and Performance Beyond Expectations.* New York: Free Press, 1985.

Bauer, M. "Are the Leadership Practices of College Presidents in the Northeast Distinct from Those of Business and Industry?" Doctoral dissertation, University of New Haven, Dec. 1993.

Berlew, D. E. "Leadership and Organizational Excitement." *California Management Review,* 1974, *17*(2), 21–30.

Berry, L. L., Parasuraman, A., and Zeithaml, V. A. "Improving Service Quality in America: Lessons Learned." *Academy of Management Executive,* 1994, 8(2), 32–45.

Blitzer, R. J., Petersen, C., and Rogers, L. "How to Build Self-Esteem." *Training and Development Journal,* Feb. 1993, 59.

Bond J. T., Galinsky, E., and Swanberg, J. E. *The 1997 National Study of the Changing Workforce.* New York: Families and Work Institute, 1998.

Borda, J. "Great Expectations." *Fast Company,* November 1999, 212–222.

Breen, B. "What's Your Intuition?" *Fast Company,* Sept. 2000, 290–300.

Buckingham, M., and Coffman, C. *First, Break All the Rules.* New York: Simon & Schuster, 1999.

Cialdine, R. B. *Influence: Science and Practice.* (4th ed.) Needham Heights, Mass.: Allyn and Bacon, 2001, 19–51.

Coffman, J. P. "The Community College Coach: Leadership Practices and Athlete Satisfaction." Doctoral dissertation, University of San Diego, Graduate School of Education, Apr. 1999.

Cohen, D., and Prusak, L. *In Good Company: How Social Capital Makes Organizations Work.* Boston: Harvard Business School Press, 2001.

Collins, J. *Good to Great: Why Some Companies Make the Leap . . . and Others Don't.* New York: HarperCollins, 2002.

Conger, J. A. "Inspiring Others: The Language of Leadership." *Academy of Management Executive,* 1991, *5*(1), 31–45.

Conger, J. A. *Winning 'Em Over.* New York: Simon & Schuster, 1998.

Cooperrider, D. L. "Positive Image, Positive Action: The Affirmative Basis of Organizing." In S. Srivastva, D. L Cooperrider, and Associates, *Appreciative Management and Leadership: The Power of Positive Thought and Action in Organizations.* San Francisco: Jossey-Bass, 1990.

Csikzsentmihalyi, M. *Finding Flow: The Psychology of Engagement with Everyday Life.* New York: Basic Books, 1997.

Deal, T., and Key, M. K. *Corporate Celebration: Play, Purpose, and Profit at Work.* San Francisco: Berrett-Koehler, 1998.

Deci, E. L. with Flaste, R. *Why We Do What We Do: Understanding Self-Motivation.* New York: Penguin Books, 1995.

Denning, S. *The Springboard: How Storytelling Ignites Action in Knowledge-Era Organizations.* Boston: Butterworth-Heinemann, 2001.

Diamond, R. M. (ed.). *Field Guide to Academic Leadership.* San Francisco: Jossey-Bass, 2002.

Driscoll, J. W. "Trust and Participation in Organizational Decision Making as Predictors of Satisfaction." *Academy of Management Journal,* 1978, *21*(1), 44–56.

Eccles, J., and others. "Self-Fulfilling Prophecies, Perceptual Biases, and Accuracy at the Individual and Group Levels." *Journal of Experimental Social Psychology,* 1998, *34*(6), 530–561.

Eden, D. "Leadership and Expectations: Pygmalion Effects and Other Self-Fulfilling Prophecies in Organizations." *The Leadership Quarterly,* 1992, *3*(4), 271–305.

El Sawy, O. A. "Temporal Perspective and Managerial Attention: A Study of Chief Executive Strategic Behavior." Unpublished doctoral dissertation, Stanford University, 1983.

Elliott, R. D. "Identifying and Analyzing the Practices Utilized by Coaches in Achieving Their 'Personal Best' in Coaching." Master's thesis, Iowa State University, June 1990.

"FC Roper Starch Survey: The Web." *Fast Company,* Oct. 1999, 302.

Gillespie, K. *A Guide to Faculty Development: Practical Advice, Examples and Resources.* Bolton, Mass.: Anker, 2002.

Goleman, D., McKee, A., and Boyatzis, R. E. *Primal Leadership: Realizing the Power of Emotional Intelligence.* Boston: Harvard Business School Publishing, 2002.

Gostick, A., and Elton, C. *Managing with Carrots: Using Recognition to Attract and Retain the Best People.* Layton, Utah: Gibbs Smith, 2001.

Grace, G. D., and Schill, T. "Social Support and Coping Style Differences in Subjects High and Low in Interpersonal Trust." *Psychological Reports,* 1986, *59,* 584–586.

Gurtman, M. B. "Trust, Distrust, and Interpersonal Problems: A Circumplex Analysis." *Journal of Personality and Social Psychology,* 1992, *62,* 989–1002.

Guskin, A. E., and Marcy, M. B. "Pressures for Fundamental Reform." In R. M. Diamond (ed.), *Field Guide to Academic Leadership.* San Francisco: Jossey-Bass, 2002.

Johnson D. W., and Johnson, R. T. *Cooperation and Competition: Theory and Research.* Edina, Minn.: Interaction, 1989.

Kaye, B. L., and Jordon-Evans, S. *Love 'Em and Lose 'Em.* San Francisco: Berrett-Koehler, 1999.

Khoshaba, D. M., and Maddi, S. R. "Early Experiences in Hardiness Development." *Consulting Psychology Journal,* 1999, *51,* 106–116.

Klein, G. *The Sources of Power: How People Make Decisions.* Cambridge, Mass.: MIT Press, 1998.

Leaming, D. R. "Academic Deans." In R. M. Diamond (ed.), *Field Guide to Academic Leadership.* San Francisco: Jossey-Bass, 2002.

LePine, J. A., and Dyne, L. V. "Predicting Voice Behavior in Work Groups." *Journal of Applied Psychology,* 1998, *83*(6), 853–868.

Lucas, A. F. "A Teamwork Approach to Change in the Academic Department." In A. F. Lucas and Associates, *Leading Academic Change* (pp. 7–32). San Francisco: Jossey-Bass, 2000.

Maddi, S. R. "Comments on Trends in Hardiness Research and Theorizing." *Consulting Psychology Journal,* 1999, *51,* 67–71.

Maddi, S. R., Kahn, S., and Maddi, K. L. "The Effectiveness of Hardiness Training." *Consulting Psychology Journal,* 1998, *50,* 78–86.

McCarty, P. A. "Effects of Feedback on the Self-Confidence of Men and Women." *Academy of Management Journal,* 1986, 840–847.

Mintzberg, H. *The Rise and Fall of Strategic Planning.* New York: Free Press, 1994.

Murphy, J. P. *Visions and Values in Catholic Higher Education.* Kansas City, Mo.: Sheed & Ward, 1991.

Nelson, R. "The Power of Rewards and Recognition." Presentation to the Consortium on Executive Education, Leavey School of Business, Santa Clara University, September 20, 1996.

Palmer, P. J. *Let Your Life Speak: Listening for the Voice of Vocation.* San Francisco: Jossey-Bass, 2000.

Plowman, R. J. "Perceptions of Presidential Leadership Behavior and Institutional Environment by Presidents and Vice Presidents of Selected Four-Year Colleges and Universities in Florida." Doctoral dissertation, University of Mississippi, School of Education, May 1991.

Poundstone, W. *Prisoner's Dilemma: John Von Neumann, Game Theory, and the Puzzle of the Bomb.* New York: Doubleday, 1992.

Public Allies. *New Leadership for a New Century.* Washington, D.C.: 1998.

Ramaley, J. A. "Moving Mountains: Institutional Culture and Transformational Change."

In R. M. Diamond (ed.), *Field Guide to Academic Leadership* (pp. 59–73). San Francisco: Jossey-Bass, 2002.

Ready, D. A. "How Storytelling Builds Next-Generation Leaders." *Sloan Management Review,* Summer 2002, 63–69.

"The Retention Dilemma" (Working paper). HayGroup, 2001.

Sawyer, J. B., Latham, W. R., Pritchard, R. D., and Bennett, W. R. "Analysis of Work Group Productivity in an Applied Setting: Application of a Time Series Panel Design." *Personnel Psychology,* 1999, *52,* 927–967.

Senge, P. *The Fifth Discipline: The Art and Practice of the Learning Organization.* New York: Doubleday, 1990.

Stephenson, S. "Promoting Teamwork: Leadership Attitudes and Other Characteristics of a Community College Chief Financial Officer." Doctoral dissertation, University of Arkansas, College of Education, May 2002.

Thackray, J. "Feedback for Real." *Gallup Management Journal,* Spring 2001, *1*(1), 12–17.

Tiger, L. "Real-Life Survivors Rely on Teamwork." *The Wall Street Journal,* August 25, 2000, B7.

Wheatley, M. *Leadership and the New Science.* San Francisco: Berrett-Koehler, 1992.

Williams, S. R., and Wilson, R. L. "Group Support Systems, Power, and Influence in an Organization—A Field Study." *Decision Sciences,* 1997, *28*(4) 911–937.

Wood, R., and Bandura, A. "Impact of Conceptions of Ability on Self-Regulatory Mechanisms and Complex Decision Making." *Journal of Personality and Social Psychology,* 1989, *56,* 407–415.

Xu, Z. L. "The Relationship Between Leadership Behavior of Academic Deans in Public Universities and Job Satisfaction of Department Chairpersons." Doctoral dissertation, East Tennessee State University, Department of Educational Leadership and Policy Analysis, May 1991.

Zipkin, A., "Management: The Wisdom of Thoughtfulness." *New York Times,* May 31, 2000, C1.

Zuboff, S. *In the Age of the Smart Machine: The Future of Work and Power.* New York: Basic Books, 1988.

INDEX

→ make a difference
(students)

① Listen for common aspirations

② Encourage everyone to speak up

③ Meaning & purpose - what does an
work give you in this regard?

④ Break down big goals into smaller
ones easier to achive
↳ review how far we've
come already

CPSIA information can be obtained at www.ICGtesting.com
Printed in the USA
BVOW03n0205070816

457861BV00007B/9/P

9 780787 966645